WOULD YOU BE WILLING?

The Story
of
Restoring The Foundations Ministry
at
Echo Mountain Inn

Also by Chester and/or Betsy Kylstra:

- Restoring The Foundations, An Integrated Approach To Healing Ministry, Chester and Betsy Kylstra, 1996.

- Twice Chosen, One Woman's Story of Healing, Betsy Kylstra, 1996.

- Biblical Healing and Deliverance, Chester and Betsy Kylstra, 2003.

- Transforming Your Business, How to Change Your Organization for Good, Chester Kylstra, 2006.

WOULD YOU BE WILLING?

The Story
of
Restoring The Foundations Ministry
at
Echo Mountain Inn

Betsy and Chester Kylstra

Restoring The Foundations Publications
Hendersonville, NC

Would You Be Willing?
The Story of Restoring The Foundations at Echo Mountain Inn

Authors: Betsy and Chester Kylstra

Published by: Restoring The Foundations Publications
               2849 Laurel Park Highway
               Hendersonville, NC 28739
               828-696-9075
               resources@RestoringTheFoundations.org
               www.RestoringTheFoundations.org

Cover Art by Mark Buchman.

First Printing, September 2017

Paperback Edition, -1, September 2017.

ISBN 978-0-9649398-0-6

TABLE OF CONTENTS

TABLE OF CONTENTS: Continued

DEDICATIONS

We want to dedicate this book to all of the Healing House Network (HHN) members who have given of their time, prayers, and resources to build the Restoring The Foundations ministry and family during our years at Echo Mountain Inn. Because of your great support, Restoring The Foundations grew from a fledgling "mom and pop" ministry to one which has become known and is respected in many parts of the world. During these years so many of our hearts have been knitted together, both in other parts of the world and around the beautiful Restoring The Foundations headquarters at Echo Mountain Inn. Thank you for growing along with us, on this great God adventure to see the Bride without spot or wrinkle.

ACKNOWLEDGEMENTS

A lot of wonderful people are a part of the story of Restoring The Foundations Ministry at Echo Mountain Inn. It is a story of God touching many lives, and also using us to touch each other.

We want to specifically acknowledge the contributions of the following people to the completion of this book, and for helping to make Restoring The Foundations the significant ministry that it has become.

This book is much richer because of personal accounts shared by: Stuart Hammond, Bob Guier, Mike Green, Susan Rhodes, David Samuels, and Lee and Cindi Whitman. Also, thank you 'Pat' for sharing the testimony of your ministry.

Julie Buchman, we greatly appreciate your labor of love in helping find the needed photographs. It was fun to re-experience this history together.

Linda Shoplock, your skill in proofreading the final draft was tremendously helpful. Thank you so much.

Paul Fitzgerald, thank you for your many years of inspirational ideas and many trips to Hendersonville to help. Thank you also for developing the Restoring The Foundations promotional video, as well as the early Restoring Your Life website. A huge thank you for creating the current RestoringTheFoundations.com website. This much needed updated website definitely moved us into the current generation. The things you have personally developed for us and Restoring The Foundations have been so instrumental in implementing our vision.

Ralph Doudra, much gratitude to you for your loving support over our years here at Echo Mountain Inn. Many lives have been touched because of what you have done behind the scenes.

PREFACE

The years 2004-2017 at Echo Mountain Inn have been crucial in the life and history of Restoring The Foundations (RTF) Ministry. These have been years of deepening relationships with each other and with God, years of internal organization, years of connecting, years of becoming recognized as a quality ministry, and years of expansion. A lot has happened in a relatively short time.

Regrets
In chronicling our story, we have only been able to include a portion of the highlights. However, regardless of the limitations of time and space, we still feel it is important to write what we can.

Our second regret is that we could not include each person who has helped make RTF Ministry what it is today. Please forgive us if your name or picture doesn't appear somewhere in this book. It was painful not to include everyone.

Many of you who are reading this book are ones who have contributed to RTF's positive growth. You have impacted lives around you, in your region, and beyond. Thank you. It is your story, combined with what has happened in and around Echo Mountain Inn, that completes the RTF story.

RTF Vision
The RTF story is primary based on the heart revelation and call to be part of God's healing army. We received this revelation and call early in our Bible College years, followed by the RTF revelation of the four sources of all of humanity's problems, followed by God's intense healing process in our lives. This healing revelation is embodied in Ephesians 5, where Paul writes:

> [25] *Husbands, love your wives, just as Christ also loved the church and gave Himself for her,* [26] *that He might sanctify and cleanse her with the washing of water by the word,* [27] *that He might present her to Himself a glorious church,* ***not having spot or wrinkle or any***

such thing, but that she should be holy and without blemish. *(Eph 5:25-27, NKJV)*

As RTF grew, we eventually put what was in our hearts into a statement of the vision for RTF Ministry.[1] Here it is:

> Restoring the Foundations provides
>   hope for healing,
>   freedom from life's deepest struggles,
>   and renewed purpose for living
> by personally experiencing (encountering) God's powerful love and peace.

As you read through this book, know every time you read the word 'vision' we are referring to the above vision statement and all that it means. It is our passion to help everyone who is willing to experience the reality of the Presence of the Living God.

Book Title

The title "Would You Be Willing?" is a phrase often heard during the months of training. The new minister is taught to ask the Ministry Receiver this question, rather than instructing him in a directive way. The phrase was said so often, that it almost became a joke.

At another level, however, this question is what God asks each one of us repeatedly. It is an explicit acknowledgement of the awesomeness of the gift of free will. And like ourselves, and the Whitmans, you and we continue to say "Yes!"

As we move into the next season in the life of RTF ministry, it seems fitting to pause and celebrate, and to give thanks for all that the Lord has done in and through our lives as we have enjoyed this ministry home for a special season. And so that is the purpose of this book. Enjoy!

---

[1] Our heartfelt "thank you" to Paul Fitzgerald for guiding us as a leadership team as he drew out the words to express what was in our hearts.

PART I
FINDING THE INN

kairos

Chapter 1
It's Time

I heard the Lord's familiar voice explode inside my spirit, words we had been waiting for; simple but powerful words containing His direction. "It's time for the Training Center."

Full and overflowing with excitement, I felt transported into the back bedroom of the cabin where Chester was still sleeping. Oblivious to the hour, with chills running up and down my spine, I began to whisper, "Honey, wake up. Something really important has happened."

As he opened sleepy eyes and squinted, my words tumbled over each other as I hurried to tell him the good news. "It's time for the Training Center. The Lord says, 'It's time, it's finally time,'" I chanted, dancing around our bed in my excitement.

Chester was not immediately excited. It was only 5 am. It was still dark outside. And as good as this news was, it did not constitute an emergency.

"Wonderful," he murmured, "can we talk about it a little later?"

My mind was racing. It was August, 2002. For over 10 years we had received prophetic words that we would have a place of our own, a ministry place to call home. After zigzagging across the states many times, as well as traveling internationally, we were more than ready to find "our place." A similar message had been repeated by many different prophets at different locations and different times. The message spoken to us went like this; "I see that the Lord is going to give you a place of your own, a place where many, many, many people can be trained, where many will be healed, and many will find their destiny. Yes, many will grow to love the Lord more in that place."

All we could say was, "Yes, Lord, let it happen. We are more than ready!"

Later that day Chester's excitement equaled mine. Holding hands we knelt on the floor of that rustic cabin and asked the Lord once again to be in charge and to show us the way, the way to finding our place, our Training Center.

It's interesting how when God gives us a big vision, it can actually make us feel quite small. The obvious truth stares us squarely in the face. Without Him, it's all quite impossible.

Chapter 2
The Search Is On

It was a little like looking for the lost coin. "Where are you, special building that will house our Training Center, that will enable all that God has spoken to us over the years? It's time to make yourself known! Would you please hurry up and come out of hiding?"

Hoping this search would go quickly, we used our unscheduled time to check out many diverse possibilities. We halfway expected to be walking on some piece of property, or looking at some building, and hear God's audible voice say, "This is it. You have found it. Congratulations!"

It didn't happen that way. No audible voice was heard. However, we did much searching to find a number of places that were **NOT** our Training Center. It wasn't a beautiful camp near San Antonio, Texas, or a hotel in Kentucky, or a site near a river in the Atlanta area. In vain, we searched for almost a year. Exhausted and discouraged, we wondered if the search was going to remain fruitless.

In July of 2003, as we sat down once again to pray about the location of 'our' Training Center, our attitudes lacked any identifiable Fruit of the Spirit. "Lord, where do You want our place to be? Where do You want it? Please tell us. We will go anywhere in the world. All we need is for You to tell us," we cried out, frustrated that there seemed to be no help from Him.

5

Almost instantly, we heard His voice. We both heard it and we both heard the same thing. It was a question right back to us. "Where do you want it?" He asked. "I have lands and buildings everywhere."

Well trained in obedience, we had never imagined that He would say that the choice could be ours. Tears trickled down our cheeks as this new reality began to sink in. He trusted us to make the choice. He had just given us permission to allow the desires of our hearts to lead us.

"Well," we asked each other, "where do we want the Training Center to be?"

"I would like to go back home to North Carolina," I blurted out.

"Oh," said Chester, looking startled. "That is a good thought. I would like to go back home to Oregon."

A rather 'warm' discussion followed. Chester ended it with, "You know, the mountains are really home to me. How would it be if we looked for our place in the mountains of North Carolina?"

As the conversation ended, we were both at peace. The area of our search was greatly narrowed; no longer the world, 'just' the mountains of North Carolina. However, you may have noticed; there are a lot of mountains in Western North Carolina. We still had a large area in which to search.

Chapter 3
"Have You Considered?"

Energy and excitement were flowing in us. We continued our ongoing discussion about what features and characteristics the Training Center must have in order to fulfill the vision. Chester was writing it all down. The list had grown to 18 points. It included, "We definitely need to be near a city with an airport."

Three days later, Chester was looking at a mapping program on his computer. He drew 25 and 50 mile radius circles around all of the airports within and near the mountains of North Carolina. He explained to the Lord, "People coming to the Training Center will need to fly into a nearby city, and we too will still be doing some travel. We have to be within a reasonable distance of an airport. However, Lord, even after I exclude all of the mountains outside these circles, there are still a lot of mountains within an hour's drive of an airport. Actually, this is still an area **way too big** for us to explore. Would You please just narrow down the search area for us?"

That same clear voice that had spoken to us earlier spoke to Chester again. "Yes, I will. Have you considered Hendersonville?"

Well, Chester had not, and we had not. We did know that this lovely town existed. We had even eaten at a restaurant there once. But, we did not KNOW Hendersonville.

We were both struck by how the Lord had phrased His statement; no demands, no ultimatums, just a simple, "Have you considered?"

Even though the choice was still very much up to us, we knew we wanted the wisdom of God guiding our decision. "Yes, Lord," Chester said, "I think we will consider Hendersonville."

Chapter 4
Unexpected Finances

The year 2003 was a fast-moving whirl-wind of a year, with many more ministry invitations than we could fulfill. We only had one unscheduled week in August. Guess where we planned to go. Yes, that is right; "Hendersonville, North Carolina."

We had our bags packed and detailed plans in hand for our search, when we received the unexpected news that my favorite uncle, Charlie Myers, had died. Immediately we headed to Greensboro, North Carolina, for his funeral before going to Hendersonville in Western North Carolina.

Sitting in the beautiful old downtown church where my grandfather had pastored for years, many memories crashed in upon me like waves rushing and tumbling onto the seashore. So many good memories; I was a six-year-old and Uncle Charlie was shaking my little hand and pressing a dollar bill into it; I was a teenager and he was mentoring me and my tennis game; I was a starving student in Europe and in his travels he would visit me bringing bags of groceries. So many tender memories. However a more recent memory lovingly settled in my mind. Uncle Charlie had let me know that he had bought a life insurance policy with me as the beneficiary and that one day I would receive an inheritance from him. So strange to realize that this was that day. This was the very time that he had talked about.

His funeral was unpretentious as he had been. This unspoiled Christian man, who had been the CEO of the largest textile company in the world, had been one of my models. "Uncle Charlie," I murmured to myself imagining that he could hear me, "I plan to use the money from that policy in a way that would make you proud. Just as you used your money to bring me life, so I will use this money to bring life to others."

Can you guess how this fits into our story?

Chapter 5
The Decision

Two strenuous days of searching in Hendersonville left us very discouraged. We threw the net out wide. We examined a church, walked through a trailer park, and looked at an old campground, as well as surveying two beautiful Inns. No property, however, jumped out at us and said, "I'm it. I'm your Training Center."

One thing, however, had become clear. Whatever property the Lord had for us was going to take some money! Not pocket change, but real money. Everything we had looked at cost well over $1 million. Some places were $2 million and more.

While we knew buying a Training Center was going to require significant funds, somehow, driving home after our week in Hendersonville, the realization of the amount of money required hit us with a new level of soberness. We rode in silence for some time, wondering, "Lord, how, just how, are You going to gather in all of this money?"

Back in Florida, we called a meeting. Our living room filled up with good friends who were also ardent prayer warriors. The Greens,[1] the Tollisons, the Thiedes, the Duenkes, the Hedmans, Dorathy Railey, and Jeannie Mack, were all there. We presented our vision to them, and that Hendersonville, NC, was the location. Then we all prayed and listened. There was a unanimous consensus. "Your vision is from the Lord. We want to

---

[1] See Mike and Michele's story in the chapter "The Green Team," page 48.

get behind it. He does own the cattle on a thousand hills. He is going to finance this vision." The vision was being birthed in our friends who were praying and believing with us. They began sharing the vision with the other RTF Healing House Network members. Soon, the funds begin to come in for the yet-to-be-found Training Center located in or near Hendersonville. The vision was growing legs and it was moving forward.

Along with the other challenges, we felt the Lord wanted us to begin to advertise the training modules we were planning for the Training Center. "What Lord?" we asked, feeling shocked. "We don't even have a specific property yet and we are just beginning to raise money." It seemed He was calling us to match our commitment to the vision with our faith. Soon the ministry's web site had an announcement on it. "Come to Restoring The Foundations Training starting August 1, 2004, in our new Training Center in the mountains of North Carolina." We were doing our best to keep our faith focused on the Lord's promises and the vision. Yet even though we did not know where the Promised Land actually was, even though it was a stretch to advertise the training at the non-existent Training Center, we still felt 100% committed.

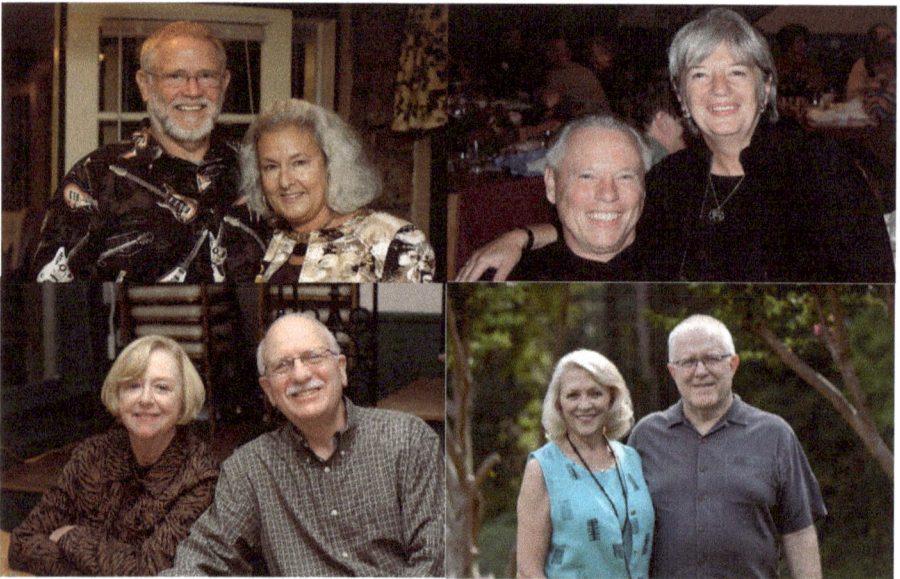

Mike and Michele Green, Rodney and Kathy Tolleson, Bob and Sue Thiede, and Ray and Emily Duenke.

Chapter 6
The Lost Coin Is Found

By December, 2003, we were heady with excitement. Love gifts were coming in for the new Training Center. We just "knew that we knew" that we would find it on this next trip to Hendersonville. As we were getting ready to leave Florida, Bishop Bill Hamon called us into his office because the Lord had given him a prophetic word for us. It included these words; "I see a big building with many, many, many rooms, with the Healing House teams ministering in them." It was awesome for the Lord to continue to encourage us onward.

Continuing our search in Hendersonville, we looked at several more possible facilities. We were beginning to feel overwhelmed with the large number of "close, but not quite right" choices.

On the Saturday before Christmas, as Chester was driving down Main Street in Hendersonville on his way to get some groceries, he had a serious talk with the Lord. "Lord," he said, "I thank You for letting Betsy and me choose the location and facilities for the new home of RTF; however, we did not realize just how many possibilities there would be here in Henderson County. We don't have time to check out every camp, hotel, motel, inn, RV park, and church for sale. Lord, I know that **You know** the very best place for us. That's the place we want to choose. Would You just tell me where it is?"

The same clear voice that we had heard before came into Chester's spirit, "Yes, it's Echo Mountain Inn. The owners are up there right now. If you go up there and talk to them, you can make a deal."

Wow! Chester immediately wondered, "Did I really hear the Lord's voice again? Did He just tell me the best place for the Training Center?"

We had visited Echo Mountain Inn (EMI) during our first trip to Hendersonville. Amazingly, it had 16 of the 18 features we had on our Features Needed List. The core part of the main building had been constructed in 1896 as a residence. Then over the years, additions had resulted in a large Inn with 22 guest rooms, a commercial kitchen, and an ambience and character that was inviting and quite unique. Three other buildings completed the setting; all in all, an ideal place for intimacy with the Lord while receiving ministry and/or training in Restoring The Foundations (RTF).

As Chester was soaking in what God had just spoken, he remembered that the owners normally closed the Inn in the winter and spent Christmas in the Florida Keys with their family. Would they really be up there "right now?"

So much for the groceries. Making a right turn onto 5th Avenue, Chester drove up the 18 curves to EMI. It would be easy to find out whether or not he had really heard the voice of the Lord.

Miracle of miracles. That year the owner's entire family had gathered at the Inn for Christmas. Three days earlier a cash deal to purchase the Inn had totally fallen through. The weary owners were more than ready to make a deal. And so were we. And so we did.

At last, the search was over! Our new home, our ministry headquarters, our Training Center to-be, had been found!

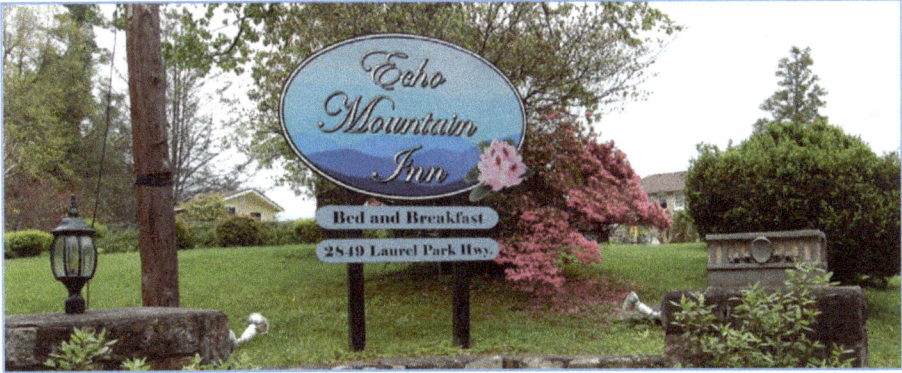

Chapter 7
Hurdles, Hurdles!

Chester and I assumed we would quickly get a loan to buy the Inn by early spring. This would give us several months to learn how to run the Inn, and to establish the curriculum and operating procedures for the Training Center. This seemed like a good and proper plan. What could go wrong?

What sounded so simple turned into a nightmare. Soon we found out we were 'non-conforming.' While our personal ministry had a good financial history, the cash flow for Echo Mountain Inn (EMI) had suffered as the owner couple had become increasingly exhausted. And so no regular bank or loan company was interested in giving us a loan; not interested at all.

After extensive searching, we did find a company that agreed to give us (the ministry) a loan. Unfortunately, their terms were horrific, essentially criminal. We realized that we had found a shifty loan shark! As terrible as the loan terms were, and as much as we wanted to just back out of the deal, the loan shark's company was the only one we had found that was willing to fund the purchase of the Inn.

By mid-May, the funds for the down payment were coming together with the help of Uncle Charlie's gift and the generosity of Restoring The Foundations (RTF) friends. However, we were still battling the lousy loan shark. His company continually failed to meet their obligation deadlines, and so the date for completing the loan processing kept being extended. While on the one hand we were grateful to have a loan, any loan, on another hand we just wanted to be rid of the loan shark, and on the third hand we felt strongly that God was going to work a miracle and bring another solution to us.

Meanwhile, time was flying by. August 1st was getting closer. Other questions needing answers were clamoring for attention: When were we to move our Florida headquarters to Echo Mountain Inn? Where were Ministry Receivers we had already committed to supposed to come for ministry? To Florida? Or to North Carolina?

"Let's rent a small apartment at Echo Mountain Inn and do ministry there," I suggested. This gave us a great opportunity to be "on site." Each day after finishing ministry, we would walk to

the gates of the property and lay our hands on them. We took time to pray and declare our prophetic words, as well as the things God had spoken directly to our hearts. We were determined to see God's promises to us and the RTF community fulfilled. Echo Mountain Inn WAS going to be the location of the RTF Training Center!

By mid-June, we were receiving many applications for the training season starting August 1st. But we still did not own a Training Center in which to hold it. The current owners were past exhausted and ready to turn the Inn over to us. "Have you heard anything about your loan yet?" they asked hopefully. The pressure was building. We really needed God to do something miraculous to salvage the situation. But what was that to be?

Chapter 8
Miracles Needed

Faithfully, Chester continued to check out every possible opportunity for a better loan. On Monday in mid-June, a bank officer casually commented, "Our bank makes commercial loans based on cash flow, however, I know of a bank in Asheville that makes loans based on collateral. Maybe they can help you."

"Cash flow," "Collateral," why hadn't someone brought this up before? Quickly Chester made an appointment for the next afternoon.

Interestingly, the loan officer who met with him started asking all kinds of questions about our ministry. Trying to be cautious, Chester replied, "I could give you a better answer if I knew what church you attend." The man's face broke into a big broad grin as he began to share his Christian experience. It had many similarities to our walk. Both men became excited. The loan officer explained, "This kind of ministry is so needed. I'll do everything I can to get your loan approved. The loan committee meets this Saturday. I will call you after the meeting."

Saturday and even Sunday slowly dragged by, moment by moment, with no telephone call. We were getting tense. It felt like one of those "You just stepped on my last nerve" scenarios.

Monday the call finally came. "Your loan has been approved," came the welcome news! And it was with very reasonable terms. Suddenly the sunshine was a little brighter. The grass was a little greener. At last we could move ahead. Our joy and relief spilled over everywhere. "Thank You, Lord." We told the story to anyone who would listen. We have to admit that a part of the joy came from telling the lousy loan shark that we didn't need him any longer. The Lord had provided a much more favorable loan.

The big hurdle that still remained in finalizing the loan was that the Inn needed to be appraised by a Commercial Appraiser. Many of us know that it takes time, much time, to find, schedule, and eventually receive an appraisal report from a Commercial Appraiser. Time was the one thing we were running out of. There were only six weeks left before August 1st and the arrival of the first Trainees. The loan officer seemed much too vague and causal about this hurdle. He did mention that he would check with a friend who was an Appraiser.

However, the very next day, as Chester was walking up to the front of the Inn, he spotted a man getting out of his car. "Can I help you?" Chester asked.

"Yes, I have been asked to appraise this Inn," he replied. "Do you know who I should talk to?"

To say Chester was surprised would be putting it way too mildly. After getting over his initial shock, he said, "Yes, I know who you should talk to. I am the one." As he begin to escort the Appraiser around the facilities, the Appraiser said, "You know, this building is so familiar. I just realized that I appraised it about four years ago. I think I still have my report with all the statistics in my office. I will just walk around and check out its condition, but I think I can get my report into your hands by next week."

"By next week?" Chester was thunder-struck! What are the possibilities of that happening, of receiving a Commercial Appraiser's report only a week after the loan was approved? Close to zero, dear friends, very close to zero. Clearly, God was in the miracle business. He wanted the Training Center ready to go by the first of August.

Our closing was on July 7th – the seventh day of the seventh month. Completeness. We now had just three weeks before the first Trainees would be arriving.

PART II
AT THE INN

Chapter 9
Powder And Paint

On July 9th, 2004, our energetic and talented transition team assembled, ready to "go for it." We needed to make the most of the three short weeks from the 'closing' to August 1st, the date set a year earlier for the start of the first training module. "God, would You help us complete all preparations needed to welcome the first class?"

While the first order of business was to convert some of the rooms to their new purposes, we also wanted to attack the deteriorated appearance of the Inn. There is an old verse that goes like this:

> A little bit of powder
> and a little bit of paint,
> makes a little bit of lady
> look a lot like what she ain't.
>
> (Author unknown)

"The Inn, yes, our wonderful Grand Old Lady Inn, looks like an old lady with no makeup," I said to Chester. Then quickly I added, "And you know that's NOT a good thing!"

Well, let's bring on the "powder and the paint" as quickly as possible. And that we did.

The atmosphere was charged with lots of energy. Although Chester and I directed people and projects, it was as if each person had come already knowing what he was to do. There was a spirit of fun, of creativity, and of hustle and bustle, as we raced against the clock to get everything ready.

Joyce Wright, a wonderful friend and community organizer, had helped me buy 28 bedspreads several weeks earlier. Although we had faith that we would indeed be purchasing the Inn, we did keep the receipts. We went with a quilt motif, the most fitting for our Grand Old Lady Inn. Pinks and greens and blues, lots of color to brighten her up.

Each member of the team brought his special gifts. Molly came from Seattle to cook. Jim and Linda Shoplock drove from New Jersey, along with all the tools of a master carpenter. Johnny and Evelyn Streett arrived from South Carolina to help with everything from carpentry to cooking. The two of them could do it all. Mark and Brenda Zeitset came as the facility and housekeeping managers. They began to work on countless overstuffed closets throwing away things that must have come over on the Mayflower. Sue Mead Stath, HHN member, brought an intern, Aggie, to manage the front desk. And then there was steady and thoughtful Chris Sherard, already elderly, but full of skill and willingness. He converted an old yucky freezer room into a Resource room where we could produce and store our publications. This took some high level converting!

During the day, we did our industrious work. We could outdo any beaver. No time was wasted. No job was considered too hard. Our greatest challenge was to set priorities: build a wall, remove the tubs, or paint? In the evenings we gathered as a community for dinner. Mostly clean, we were more than ready to eat. Often we would pray for our work, for the coming Trainees, and that nothing God wanted to do in our new place would be derailed. We also prayed for a special need. Jim Shoplock had advanced cancer. He wanted to serve God, giving his skills during his last days. We prayed for healing, as well as for strength to get through each day.

Our four highest priorities became: 1) to turn the downstairs, a bar/party area, into Classroom One, 2) to turn one of the four buildings at Echo Mountain Inn, which had been converted into a home, into a Training Center, with separate training rooms and enough bathrooms, 3) to establish the resource/publications room, 4) to convert the fourth building, a smoke-stained, smelly little guesthouse/apartment, into a workable administrative office. Taken together, this was a tall order for our small crew to accomplish in three weeks.

Linda helped in every capacity. At this time, we did not know that she would return by herself and become an indispensable teacher and trainer.

The house, where the previous owners had lived, was quickly transformed into the Training Center. It's amazing what a sign with a new name can do! Walls were torn down and new ones built. Old bathtubs were hauled out to the tune of some back strain. A corner kitchen became a usable office space (and eventually, our prayer room). Stained rugs and torn padding were jerked out, rolled up, and hauled away. And then the powder and paint began. We just barely finished painting one downstairs ministry room the night before we needed it for training. This tear-down and rebuilding process was being repeated at several locations throughout the buildings.

Our administration building took equal amounts of prayer and coats of 'Kilz' to stop the intense smoke smell. Literally, everything had to be replaced; furniture, drapes, carpet, and

pictures. It had absorbed the smoke chemicals from three years of rentees who were heavy smokers. Hauling it away, we wondered, "Could this nasty place really be made useable?"

Classroom One had a curious shape, with a "back area" used for storage. "Which area should be the front of the room," we wondered? And it seemed so dark. "Paint it yellow," we all agreed. And so with rollers and brushes and paint-stained shirts, we tackled it, creating a very pleasant usable space.

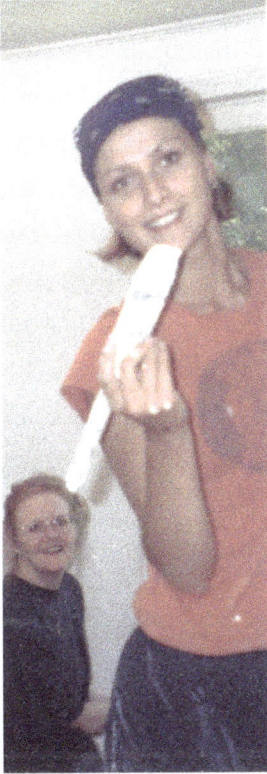

The three weeks whipped by. As the last day came, we were finishing the last tasks. It was hard for us to accept that the time had come to part ways. So much had been done, so many creative ideas had been implemented. Pushing ourselves to the limit, we had all been part of an amazing team, a team with one heart and purpose, a team that was making things happen. We had lumps in our throats as we said, "Goodbye." It was especially hard saying 'Goodbye" to Jim and Linda, knowing how sick Jim was.[1]

This was the first round of many RTF hugs and tears. In the years to come, this would be a common part of the shared experience at Echo Mountain Inn.

Our Grand Old Lady was being transformed. She was adapting beautifully for our new purposes. Her foundations were being cleaned and greatly strengthened. The powder and paint were working absolute wonders. She looked ready to begin a new dance. And for the first time, a deep sense of peacefulness was beginning to permeate the atmosphere.

---

[1] Sadly, Jim passed away the end of December.

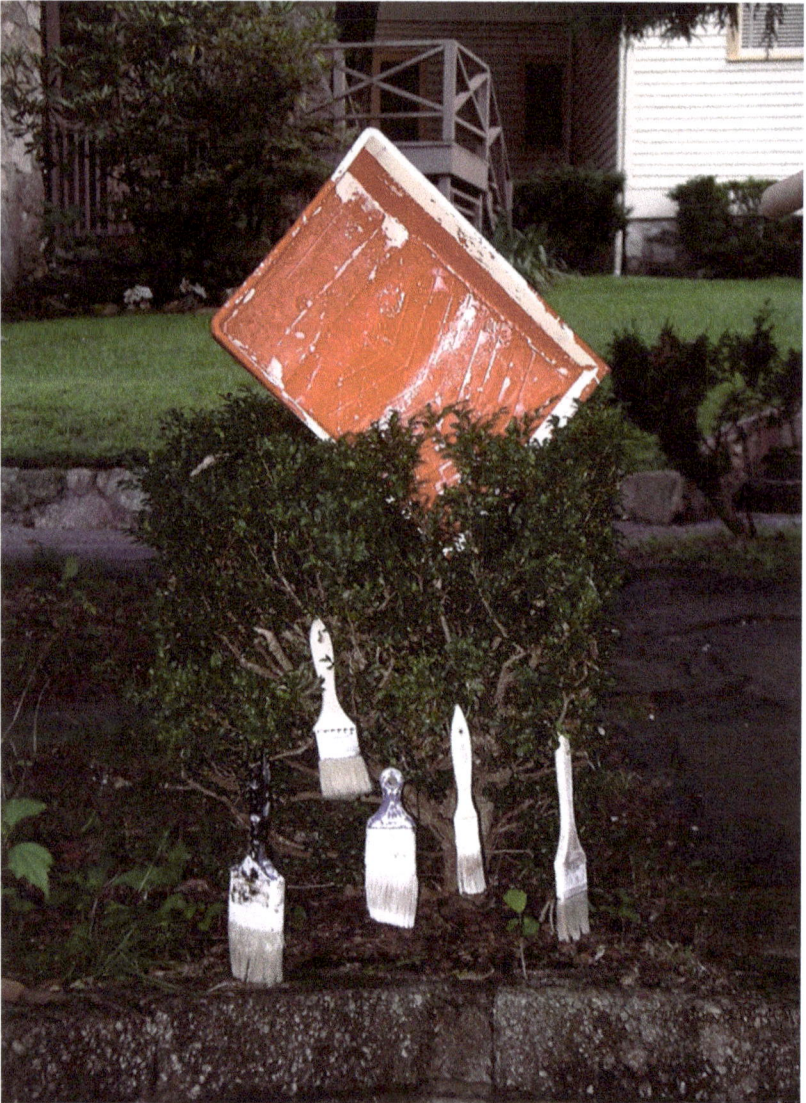

Paint brushes drying as the first trainees arrive.

Chapter 10
Early Beginnings

Here we were in our mid-60s, about to take another giant leap. Chester and I had never run a Training Center before, although I had been the director of a para-professional training program at a community college, and Chester had taught many years at the University of Florida. Neither had we run an Inn, although we did manage a four-bedroom motel unit while at Christian International in Florida. Many people stayed there for a week while they received RTF ministry from us or from one of the other ministry teams.

As we contemplated the challenges ahead, a funny memory came back to us. In our early years, a good friend had taken on the challenge of building a very complicated home. One day we asked him, "Bill, have you ever built a house before?" "Oh yes," he said confidently, "I built a birdhouse once!" Bill went from building a birdhouse to a complex four-bedroom home. We were making the same type of leap, from a four-bedroom motel to a 33 guestroom Inn. In addition, we were taking a giant step going from teaching 15 hour seminars to a Training Center curriculum covering five months, with many teams being trained simultaneously. Can you hear the sounds of "STRETCH?"

The good news was that our faith and trust had grown as we so clearly saw God's fingerprints all over so many miraculous events leading up to this time. We moved forward with a very deep and abiding sense of purpose. "Here goes something," I was fond of saying, but I knew He was behind us.

Early in the summer of 2004, Chester and I agreed that I was to be the Training Center Director and he would help me as well as take care of the "back office" work. We felt our respective giftings would be best expressed with this arrangement. A flurry of work took place as I pulled together our very first curriculum.

As August 1st came, our Trainees began arriving. Fresh and eager to begin, they were totally unperturbed by the two bathtubs still lying on the ground outside the Training Center. Preparation and transformation work was still going on. Somehow, we were always able to finish a room at least one day before it was needed.

First, we welcomed Agnieszka, a young woman from Poland who came by way of Elam Bible College. Interestingly, as I was picking up her application to review it, the Lord spoke to my heart, "Take this one, no matter what the cost." It didn't take long to discern her passion for God, her excellent mind, and her desire to serve. A lifelong bond was formed with Agnieszka, and later with her family.

Katerina and Agnieszka

Then, Katerina came from Slovakia, three ladies from the West Indies, and a wonderful couple Kate and Gordon from the UK. From Singapore came Pastor David Lee, Daniel, and Deborah Ng, eager to learn RTF ministry and take it back to Asia. Leaving their beautiful home in Hawaii, Richard and Ann Nolan arrived, with Ann in a wheelchair. The class was completed with a number of very gifted Americans. We felt God was bringing us His best.

As we looked around at that first class, our eyes were misty. This was it. This was our beginning, the fulfillment of the vision God had given to us.

In all, seven people came from other nations. At one time we had felt the Lord said to call our Training Center the "International Training Center." We felt reluctant to do so – but now we saw why. He was going to send people from all over the world. "Okay, Lord, 'International' it is!" And so we dove in.

As we began our long-awaited venture, Mike and Michele Green, Sue Mead Stath, and ourselves made up the first training staff. Classroom One (we actually had only one classroom) had a podium, a few pictures on the wall, very hard chairs, and a smell of fresh paint. In spite of the smell, it was working. Lives were being touched.

The goal of Training Module I, weeks one and two, was to qualify a person to lead the Issue-Focused Ministry, the 'three' hour version of RTF. As everyone concentrated on the training, it was exciting to see God use the publications He had had us develop in the late 90s. There was the blue Ministry Leader's Guide, the yellow Ministry Receiver's Guide, and the white Seminar Observer's Guide. Even though these publications would continue to be refined in the coming years, the people in Classroom One were being gloriously healed as they followed the procedure laid out in the publications.

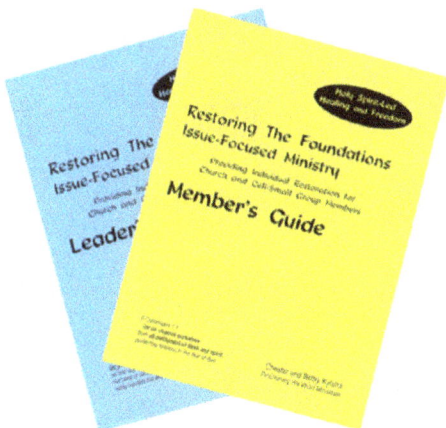

During those very first weeks of training, we put in place several elements that would become permanent parts of the RTF training. First, we determined to start each morning with worship, a devotional, and prayer. We wanted to ensure that a God focus would set the stage for each day. In addition, we instituted a Celebration Meal at the end of each training module. This was a much anticipated time, with bright table settings, vulnerable

29

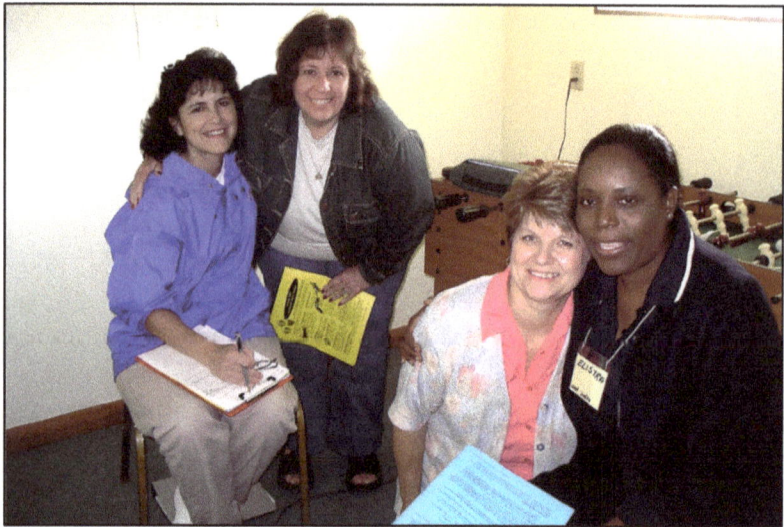

testimonies, gourmet food, good messages, skits and communion. It was a final recognition of people's growth and hard work, gratitude, and bonding. Hugs and more tears. "Don't forget to text me and see when we can get together," was repeatedly expressed. The Celebration Meal was a keeper.

It seemed as if the Inn itself gathered her big arms around all of us, and brought a quiet but substantial sense of unity. There were tears as people left her and left each other, starting with the first Module I. With the Lord's help, we had made the leap.

Chapter 11
The God Factor

How on earth would anyone find his way to a little-known ministry in the mountains of Western North Carolina? This is something Chester and I wondered about more than once. Well, move over and make way for the supernatural!

Listen, for example, to the testimony of the pastor's wife from the West Indies whom I mentioned earlier. As Training Module I was drawing to a close, she asked us, "Would you be interested in hearing how I got here?" "Yes, of course!" We were all ears.

About three months ago I had a dream. In this dream I saw an old, broken down temple. I felt huge sadness to see this temple in such devastation. For the next several days I could not get this dream off my mind. I kept pondering what the Lord was trying to tell me. As I prayed, I kept hearing the word 'restored' or maybe 'restoring.' I felt it had something to do with a book, so I went to Amazon.com to search for those words. I found your book, *Restoring The Foundations*. As I looked at the web page, I realized that the picture on the cover was the exact same broken-down temple I had seen in my dream! Immediately I called my husband and let him know this was a divine connection. I had been praying about how to bring a counseling program into our church, and here the Lord had led me to a counseling/healing ministry called "Restoring The

Foundations." My heart was pounding with excitement as I told my husband, "I have to go to this ministry." And that is how I got here. It has been a life changing two weeks for me and the two ladies who came with me.

We marveled at her story.

Each Trainee who came was special. We who were RTF Staff delighted in pouring into them during their stay. Almost every year there were stories of God speaking to people about their coming to Western North Carolina to get trained in RTF.

Here is another example of God directing a couple to us for training. We had met this lovely American couple during one trip to Toronto. We were both attending a Father's Heart conference at the Toronto Airport Christian Fellowship. Having an opportunity to pray for them, we also told them about the RTF Training Center in NC.

Sometime later, as we were approaching the start of a new training season, their names kept coming to me. Every day for almost a week, I thought of them. Finally, on Sunday evening, I asked Chester if he remembered that "Ed and Sue Moraski" couple we had met in Toronto, and if he had any contact information for them. To my surprise, he replied that he had also been thinking of them, and felt we were to contact them and remind them of the upcoming training. It was rare for us to feel we should directly encourage someone to come for training. However, in this instance, we decided to take a risk and do it. Chester quickly located their phone numbers.

At 6 o'clock that evening, I hesitantly made the call. A man answered who said he was Ed, but when I said who I was, he sounded more like someone who was in shell shock. "Oh no," I pondered, "What could be the matter?" Quickly I said, "Maybe this isn't a good time for you to talk. What if I call you again later in the evening?" "Yes," he stammered, "call back in about an hour."

At seven when I tried again, Ed and Sue were both on the phone. This is what they shared.

For the past month we have been praying about coming to your Training Center at Echo Mountain Inn. We just couldn't get a certainty about whether we should come or not. Finally, in some frustration, this afternoon we decided to put out a 'fleece.' This was our fleece. "If the Kylstras themselves call us in the next 48 hours, we will know we are supposed to go." We had just settled into a time of listening prayer when you called. We were so shocked at how quickly our 'fleece' had been answered that we couldn't even talk!

Then it was our turn to be shocked. "It would seem that maybe you are supposed to come," we stammered.

And so, the "Ed and Sue Moraski" couple showed up and took full advantage of their time of training. Later, as staff, they provided Restoring The Foundations ministry at Randy Clark's Global Awakening school in Pennsylvania. Now just how glorious is that?!

The people the Lord sent to us supernaturally came from many different places in the world. We will never forget how God spoke to a couple in Scotland. Here is their account in their words.

A Vision Given
Stuart Hammond

It came during the morning worship at the Edinburgh Vineyard Church, Scotland, UK, in 2003.

God downloaded a very clear picture of a dilapidated Roman Temple, with a sense that this represented the church and that Christ wanted to "Heal His Bride." This was followed by hearing the words, "Restoring the Foundations." At first I wondered if the pastor had spoken the words, but then I realized God had spoken. All the while, I was encompassed by God's enduring passion to bring healing to His church.

This sort of thing had never happened to me before. I was very puzzled and awed by it all. So when Helen and I arrived home after church, we decided to search for the "Restoring The Foundations" words with Google. I nearly fell off the chair when up popped the very same picture God had given me – on the front cover of the Restoring The Foundations book!

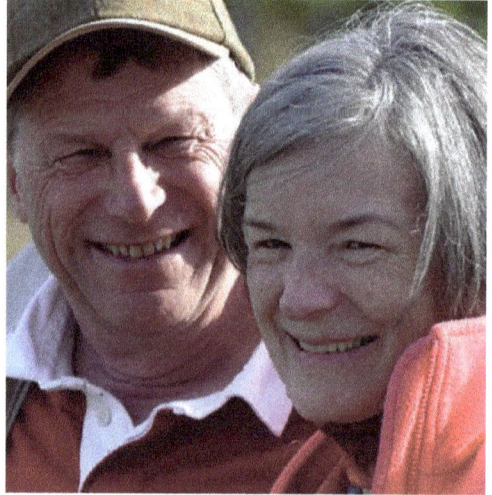

There followed several years of trying to find out where and how training might be available for us. We spoke to Ian and Olive McMichael, a RTF Healing House Team in Scotland, however, they were not doing training. Finally, in the fall of 2006, we were able to attend the first level of training, the Issue-Focused Ministry, in Bath City Church in South England.

During the years we were looking for a training opportunity, I received another vision of an unfinished building project (much like you see in Greece). It was a rectangular box-shape with holes where windows would one day be fitted. The sense accompanying this was that God wanted us to bring color and life to the buildings through praise and worship.

To our immense surprise, while at the IFM training at Bath City Church, a new book from Chester and Betsy was introduced, titled "Transforming Your Business." Again, I nearly fell off my seat, as the picture on the cover of the book was very much like the vision I had seen. It seemed that God wanted to confirm that we were in the right place!

As a brief background to these events, Helen and I had met through Christian Connections following the breakdown of our first marriages. Helen had been very wounded by the church, having been married to a minister for about 20 years. My early childhood was in the Exclusive Brethren, followed by the Open Brethren, then Baptist, and then Church of England.

I was 60 years of age before I was finally able to pursue my heart vision for RTF. I had to retire from the Forces. Helen had a good job with the NHS, but she was able to request an early retirement at age 58 so that both of us could train together.

Although we had received UK RTF IFM training in 2006, our Vineyard church in Edinburgh had not released us to do RTF ministry. Yet our hearts continued to be called into this ministry. So we decided to go to the USA to receive training at the source, at the RTF International Training Center. We showed up in January, 2010, to attend all three modules.

We had been living in a caravan (small travel trailer) for six months while our 160 year old cottage was undergoing major re-modelling. As we left, there was 12" of snow on the ground and we had been told to pack some summer clothes! Finding what we needed before time to leave was a challenge.

We did okay in Training Module I, since we had had the earlier training in IFM. However, as we progressed into Modules II and III, the program demands increased. God dug deeper to bring up our former woundings. We found ourselves regularly in the queue for more ministry!

Overall, we found the schedule extremely challenging. Only after we had been back home for a number of months did we realize just what God had done in us. We became VERY thankful for all the work/ministry that was done on our behalf by the RTF Trainers and support staff. We are amazed at the quality and maturity of training and ministry available to the students at Echo Mountain Inn. We feel it is likely impossible to replicate this depth of change outside of the USA. We feel truly blessed to have been able to attend the RTF training at Echo Mountain Inn!

It has been a long, slow process as we have finally entered our "Promised Land" as RTF Healing House Network members. God continues to stretch us with complex ministry opportunities. For example, we have had more folks presenting with mental health issues in 2017, although, we continue to help couples with their marriages more than other aspects of the ministry.

We even have a place now to minister to people. Through patiently waiting on God's timing and provision, the work of developing a former animal byre into a beautiful ministry room has been completed.

(Continue Kylstras...) Just to think that we had been concerned about people finding their way here. We had underestimated the God Factor. The 'supernatural' had become the 'natural.'

Chapter 12
Sights And Sounds Of Community

"Hurry up, hurry up, you will be late for worship," people called to each other, scrambling to gather everything needed for the long day's activities.

In the early years, our anointed 'family' led live worship. We were so blessed to have Susan Rhoads at the keyboard, or Jaqie Orsi with her guitar. When Mike Green came, he would lead with *Thank You Lord* or *Misty Mountains* (I humbly offer You my will). Each one could take us into true worship. Each one helped us focus and remember that we were truly on a God adventure.

We, Mike and Michele Green, and Sue Mead Stath were the initial teachers/trainers for the very first Training Module I. It was so much fun overseeing the new Trainees in their small groups. As they followed the Issue-Focused Ministry guidelines, the Holy Spirit was faithful, bringing healing to the ones receiving ministry. In the following years we recruited Richard and Ann Nolan, Bob and Sue Thiede, and Brian and Linda Jacobson to help us as small group leaders.

Richard and Ann Nolan, Brian and Linda Jacobson

Is it an understatement to say that many of our Trainees had a full-blown case of the jitters as they practiced leading the IFM with each other? Going through the four ministry areas plus forgiveness, they soon learned the most important lesson of all; "God will even use little ol' me; even me with my jitters; even me when I get on the wrong page of the book; even me when I have the same hurting places as my Ministry Receiver. God led me. He came through." What a turning point for our Trainees.

Trust flourished between people as vulnerable places in our lives were exposed to each other, and treated with respect and kindness by the ones ministering. God always came through. The oversight Trainers watched and listened diligently. They were careful to only intervene for a 'teaching moment,' or to correct as needed. This soon became the familiar flow of events that happened every year.

When people worship together, clean the kitchen together, minister to and with each other, and hear each other's 'dark' secrets, there is something that happens. It's a lot like being in the trenches together. People learn to cover each other's backs. Lifelong friendships are developed. We call it community.

For example, one woman moved all of the way from Raleigh, NC, to Sydney, Australia, to help her former classmates do needed administration work. Another woman flew from Sweden to Georgia to be a bridesmaid in her classmate's wedding. In the summer of 2017, a group of nine classmates, who knew and loved each other, met in Mozambique to offer special Issue-Focused Ministry to Iris ministry leaders.

One particular expression of community that stands out occurred with the class of 2014. Every Friday night the class members chose to gather to prepare and share their meal. Afterward, they taught and shared among themselves. It was one of those powerful times of bonding.

Often there was a much enjoyable sense of purpose and comradery among the teachers and Trainers. We joined in sharing not only in the training process, but also felt like midwives birthing another class of effective ministers. We all had a part in the Trainees' success. Community among the Restoring The Foundations Trainers thrived.

Soon into the training years, we were a bit shocked to realize that our influence as Trainers far surpassed what we had taught in the classroom. Many times the Trainees reported that the thing that had impressed them the most was how much the couples here loved and respected each other. For some, this was a turning point, which resulted in their having a new picture of marriage, and later enabled them to marry.

And so for five months out of each year, our Grand Old Lady made herself totally available for our intensive but life-giving training process. For thirteen years she provided a warm and safe atmosphere for life-long community to form.

Chapter 13
A Healing Community

Chester and I knew from the beginning that our call was to establish the RTF International Training Center but not to be its directors forever. We were to get it started by creating the training materials and curriculum, and to establish the training process. Then we were to raise up and mentor other teams who had the heart and the ability to become training center directors. As these teams matured, we were to select one to become the International Training Center's directors. As we did this, several teams were matured and started regional Training Centers (for example, in the UK, Canada, West Coast, and in Singapore).

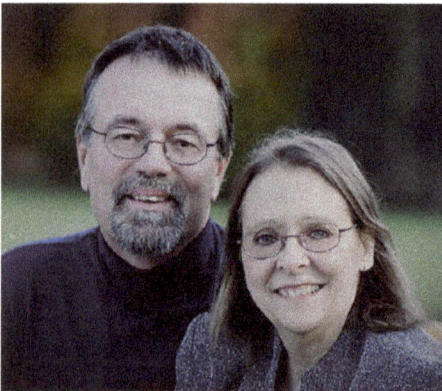
Bob and Cheria Guier

One of these teams was Bob and Cheria Guier. We knew when we first met them that there was something very special about them. We sensed that God would use them greatly with Restoring The Foundations, although we did not know exactly how at that time. Gradually, as we learned of their many giftings, we realized they had the potential to become the International Training Center Directors. And so we mentored them for this purpose. We still laugh about all the "midnight meetings" we had together, praying and problem solving sensitive issues.

As Directors, Bob and Cheria played a major role during the decade of the rapid development of RTF. Many Trainees and Trainers have incubated and grown under their dedicated leadership. Thank you, Bob and Cheria. We deeply appreciate what you have contributed as you have poured your lives into so many people, and as you have

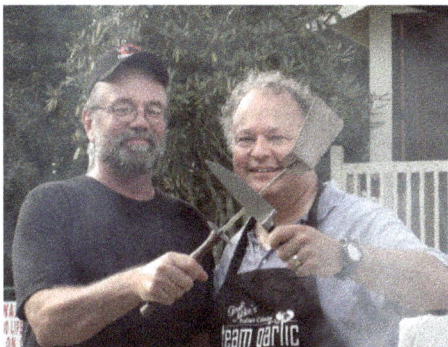
Bob Guier and Mike Best

helped update the training materials and refined the training process. Thanks too for all of the turkeys you smoked and game you cooked for the whole community to enjoy.

What Bob shares in his Reflections is a description of the deepest level of personal relationship change that many have experienced during their time of training. What could be more significant? God had done more in people's lives than we could have ever imagined.

Friends, be inspired as you read Bob's Reflections.

Reflections
Bob Guier

If the International Training Center (ITC) in Hendersonville, North Carolina, could possibly be summed up in one word, it would be this – Relationship. Authentic Relationship. Not surface relationship, which is standard fare at conferences and seminars and most often causes us to feel passed over and ignored, like someone is looking right through us. And certainly not spiritual or business relationship, which is used for corporate maintenance of programs and 'to do' lists.

The Relationship found at the ITC was neither surface nor businesslike. It was an intimate and heart-to-heart relationship.

41

Relationship: where a small group of people could feel safe enough to reveal themselves emotionally in front of each other.

Relationship: where hearts blended with one another, where lives mixed with one another leading to a mingling of souls.

Relationship: that makes us feel alive, like we've been found, as if someone finally took the time to peer into the depths of our soul and really see us there.

Relationship at the ITC began on the first day of classes with the foundational truth that our main job as RTF Ministers is to set the table for the Ministry Receiver to meet his Father God. These were just mere words at the start of each module for the Trainees. But after each ministry week, as every RTF Trainee continuously witnessed divine encounters between the Ministry Receiver and his Heavenly Father, the Trainees experientially discovered the foundational truth was indeed … TRUE. Every divine encounter changed hearts, changed lives, changed relationships.

The Trainees learned that real Relationship with Father God was the basic building block all the other facets of ministry rested on. And knowingly or not, they then applied this same principle to their other relationships at the ITC, with fellow Trainees and RTF Staff. This process did not happen overnight with everyone. Just as every snowflake is unique, almost every person at the ITC grew relationally in proportion to his own personal healing.

This heart-to-heart Relationship manifested itself in two very wonderful and powerful ways.

First, the Trainee's Relationship with God
Trainees and Trainers spent almost every day and almost every waking hour with each other, eating, working, playing, crying, laughing, cleaning toilets, washing dishes, worshipping, "howling at the moon,"

and all the other routines of everyday life. Life at the ITC wasn't an 8-5 job, it was a 24/7 family commitment.

After a passage of time in this environment, both Trainees and Trainers eventually tired of the game of maintaining a false appearance and decided to take off their masks and became real with each other. They revealed their warts, unhealed hurts, idiosyncrasies, dreams, and visions. They now knew the good, the bad, and the ugly about each other. But they all chose to not judge each other's frailties, but rather become defenders of each other's weaknesses, even knowing what they knew about each other.

This was a life situation many Trainees had not experienced before. For the first time, many of them felt safe with an authority figure; in this case, their Trainers. With feeling 'safe' came the ability to trust that their Trainers actually did have their best interests at heart.

Almost all the ITC Trainees received a good deal of life-changing personal ministry from very experienced Trainers during their time at the ITC. Gifted and experienced Trainers gladly and selflessly invested blood, sweat, and tears into the Trainees' healing. In turn, the Trainees put their pride aside, they turned off their defense mechanisms, and they willingly made themselves vulnerable. They trusted their Trainer's ability to help bring them back from the very depths of life's deepest hurts into the safe, healing, and loving Presence of their Father God.

As the Trainees received healing, their levels of trust and faith in 'The Giver of Life' blossomed into a fruitfulness that surprised even themselves. But most importantly, this Relationship with their Father God became more personal than many had ever before experienced.

Second, Trainers' Relationship with their Trainees
Each and every Trainer at the ITC had a very narrow and focused purpose – to help the Trainees become the very best RTF Minister they could be. And every Trainer made choices that required huge personal sacrifices to fulfill that purpose.

Training at the ITC did not stop at the end of a normal work day, at 5:00 pm, Monday through Friday. Most times throughout the modules, training occurred six days a week and went from 7:00 am until midnight on many nights. During these training hours, the Trainer would take the Trainees under his wing and patiently and gently invest and impart insights, wisdom, and most especially, personal feedback harvested from many years of experience.

Because of the ever-present and watchful involvement of the Trainers, the Trainees were constantly exposed to new anointings and ministerial nuances that can only be caught, not taught. The Trainers' constructive and insightful feedback facilitated the Trainees developing their own individual strengths and overcoming their weaknesses.

Through the Trainers, advanced training was given, guidance working with the Holy Spirit was modeled and encouraged, and a much deeper understanding/ comprehension of the RTF ministerial concepts and principles was achieved. The cumulative effect was to produce Ministers capable of very, very effective ministry.

Because Relationships of trust and safety were established between the Trainers and Trainees, the Trainees allowed the Trainers who believed in them to stretch them beyond their comfort zone right into their God-given potential. As a result of their Trainers' challenges and mentorship, the Trainees were able to use their ministerial abilities and giftings to a fruitfulness most Trainees had not before imagined or even realized.

The reasons these results could come about were many, but they all rested on the foundation of intimate and heart-to-heart Relationship, first with God, then with each other.

The Trainees learned about and personally experienced different aspects of Relationship during their time at the ITC. And as each graduating class was released to the world, each and every one of them were carriers of God's Presence that was birthed out of reborn, renewed, and reinvigorated Relationship with Him.

Today, as we hear the stories and testimonies of RTF Ministers here in America and elsewhere outside of our borders, it doesn't take long to see that the Trainees of years past have taken up the torch and are blowing the embers of real Relationship upon all those who cross their paths. The ITC graduates have moved from the role of receiving life at the ITC to the role of giving life to a hurt and lonely world devoid of real relationship. Thus, many ITC graduates as well as RTF Ministers who couldn't attend the ITC, are making a difference in the world, helping cleanse the spots and wrinkles from the Bride's dress, preparing Her for the return of Her awesome and wondrous Bridegroom.

As Cheria and I reflect back on the countless warm and inspiring memories we have of all who crossed the threshold of the doors of the ITC during our tenure as directors, one thought is indelibly etched in our minds and hearts: It truly was an honor and a privilege to be a part of the lives of every single RTF International Center Trainee that Father God entrusted into our care for a short season of their lives.

Stephan and Francine Heiks, Sherry Douglas and Lewis Smith, Barry and
Sandra Falkenstine, JoAnna Goodwin Ahmad, Sonja Underwood, Mike and
Phyllis Best, Daryl and Lynn Hovey, and Dan and Ruanne Banse.

(Continue Kylstras...) Our love and appreciation also go to many others, who for a number of years have given of themselves here at the ITC to advance the vision. These include the Greens, Sue Mead Stath, Nolans, Jacobsons, Tollesons, Heiks, Linda Shoplock, Falkenstines, Sherry Douglas, Sonja Underwood, Bests, Hoveys, JoAnne Goodwin Ahmad, and Banses. Some of these, such as Linda, have volunteered hundreds of hours in ministry, committed to seeing our Trainees become all that they can be. Of course we also taught at times, but we were more interested in making room for others.

Chapter 14
The Green Team

Perhaps it is time to further introduce Mike and Michele Green, or the "Green Team," as we affectionally call them.

Our lives collided with Mike and Michele way back in the 1980s. Unlike most collisions, this one had a positive outcome, positive for the next 30 plus years. Mike and Michele were the very first couple we asked to join us in the ministry. They moved from St. Augustine to the Gulf Coast of Florida. Through the depth and effectiveness of their ministry, they were a major factor in the good reputation gained by RTF in the early years.

Mike and Michele were the ones we first told about our vision for a Training Center. They quickly understood the plan and joined us in our excitement. Initially, we all assumed "Of course!" they were supposed to move with us to where the Training Center would be. But as they prayed, they heard a divine "No."

It was probably a good thing they stayed in Florida, since the surf never rises very high in Hendersonville! However, they said to us, "We are not supposed to move, but we will come and help you in any way you need us."

Need them? Of course we needed them. They have been 100% faithful to that promise to the tune of putting over 100,000 miles on their cars. They have taught and trained and Mike has led worship. They have come for all the Celebration Meals. We could not have asked for more.

Michele is known as an excellent trainer. Her Trainees are among the most proficient ministers in the HHN. She also never gets too far away from her favorite health food; 'Chocolate.' She is also good at getting the last word. If you ever say, "Michele, I love you." her come back is, "I love you more." Over the years, many people have felt "loved more" by both of the Greens.

Mike is a theologian, thoughtful and thought-provoking. His thrust in life, as well as Michele's, is to walk closely with their God. Mike's books are so worth reading. Both *Effective Listening* and *Life with God* are a must.

In some ways, Mike and Michele have been informal chaplains for the RTF Healing House Network, as many have gone to them for ministry and personal help. Along with us, they also helped mentor Bob and Cheria Guier as they became the ITC Directors. Mike and Michele, "Thank you." We wouldn't have wanted to do this RTF vision without you.

Hear Mike's heart as he shares with you his experience of being part of RTF.

Scenes From Echo Mountain Inn
Mike Green

Prelude To Scene One

The pale golden sunlight was breaking the eastern horizon as I walked across the cool damp beach. I could see through the early morning haze that the surf was breaking well. Not too big to be threatening, but not so small to be disappointing. All the essential elements of nature were in harmony. Wind, tide, and swell, dancing together in an inviting display of cosmic unity. I knew from decades of experience this was going to be one of those wonderful mornings when my years of persevering in the art of surfing were to be rewarded. Once again I was alone on my beach, not another living soul in sight and I was about to enter my favorite prayer closet.

As I knelt on the coarse golden sand to apply a fresh coat of wax to the deck of my board my thoughts had already turned to God. Ever aware of His Presence, I am also continually thankful for His provision through the years. "Thank you, Lord," I said quietly. Inwardly I felt the thrill of deep peace and contentment. I stood up cradling my board under my right arm and smiled as the third wave of a good set broke, sending white spray rushing into the air like translucent lace, suspended above the green water for a moment until vanishing into the ether.

The chilly water encased my body as it covered first my feet, then my legs and finally my torso. The sand of the seabed softly massaging my bare toes was a familiar pleasure. I took a deep breath in through my nose and dove forward under a crashing wave. "Ahh," I signed inwardly, "submerged in the sea again, encased in the salt water of my friend, the ocean."

Emerging from the invigorating rinse I popped up onto my surfboard and paddled out toward the sandbar beyond the breaking waves. After several minutes of work dodging waves, duck diving, and paddling hard, I reached the zone, and sat up on my board. The orange ball of fire was breaking the horizon now filling the pale blue sky with streams of radiant light. Once again I heard my voice speak aloud, "Ahh, Lord God, you have made the heavens and the earth with your Great Power!"

After a few minutes sitting in the silence, I picked a good wave, turned and flopped down on my board and began paddling toward shore. As the wave crested I rose to my feet, feeling the glorious moment of weightlessness as my board fell down the slope of the wave. I leaned into the wave's face, left foot forward, and my board responded immediately. Like being shot out of a gun my board and I flew across the vertical wall of the wave, first low off the bottom, then up and across the lip. Down again into the pit and then off and up along the top. As we rushed shoreward I trailed my right hand on the lip of the wave. "Ah yes, this is surfing!"

"How many times, how many years, how many decades, have we been doing this?" I asked my silent Companion as I paddled back toward the lineup, the familiar surge of joy tingling every nerve in my body. "The joy of riding waves never fades." Instantly flooding back into my mind I saw places, and faces, and waves, and beaches, memories from more than five decades of "paddling out."

Reaching the take-off spot I sat up facing the morning sun and again, thanked God.

"Thank You, Lord God. Thank You for Your unmerited favor, Your love, Your patience and provision, for Your protection, and for my healthy body. You are truly amazing and I love you more than words can express!"

I sat there rocking quietly in the gentle undulating rhythm of the sea, awaiting the next wave. My mind turned toward my next trip north to Hendersonville. I was leaving the following morning before dawn, driving the five hundred miles north to Echo Mountain Inn and the ITC one more time. "How many times have I made that drive? How many miles of pavement have passed beneath my wheels?" Thoughts of countless times I made the drive came flooding to the surface of my mind. I saw the faces of people from all over the globe. From England, Switzerland, Germany, Poland, Israel, Sri Lanka, Singapore, South Africa, Australia, New Zealand, China, Japan, Brazil, Panama, Mexico, and Canada. Shaking my head in amazement I blurted out, "Wow! Lord." Then I thought of the line from that movie, "If you build it they will come." And I heard another line, one from the Bible, "Eye has not seen, ear has not heard, nor has it entered the mind of man, all that God has provided for those who love Him and answer the call into His service."

Scene One

More than ten years ago I walked through the parking lot of Echo Mountain Inn in the dark before the dawn. The sun had not risen, the eastern sky had not yet begun to lighten. The property was dark, the birds silent, and the garbage-seeking bears had retreated to their beds. As I prayed and spoke with God about this place He had given to Chester and Betsy, I heard Him say, "Echo Mountain Inn is now functioning in the role that I originally intended for it. No one comes onto this property but by divine appointment." I thought, "Really?"

Then I saw a vision of an old photo album. It was one of those black rectangular books with flimsy covers. The edges were curled from years of being turned. As I gazed upon the book the cover opened and the pages began to turn slowly as if by an unseen hand. The photos were old, black and white, faded, and some of their corners were bent or torn. The people in the photos were posing in various rooms, porches, and lawns around the property. They were dressed in the fashions of bygone eras. The album was a collection of photos of different periods of time beginning in the late 1800's and continuing up to the present time. But what made it odd was even the photos which appeared to have been taken recently looked old; they were black and white, faded, cracked, like the older ones.

As I gazed more closely on the photos I began to realize a very amazing thing. The people in the photos were people I knew from my time at the ITC, even the people in the oldest photos.

He said, "You are seeing the history of the Inn from a future perspective." I had somehow been transported into the future and was looking back on the present. The more recent scenes and familiar faces of the people appeared old and charming, in a heartwarming way.

Scene Two
Recently as I was praying about the future of the Inn He spoke again. "The Inn has accomplished My Will. I gave it to them for My purpose and My purpose has been fulfilled. Those who have come have come at My invitation. Some have stayed briefly, while others have stayed much longer. My Will has been encountered by each one. Chester and Betsy bought the Inn because I asked them to buy it. Now I have asked them to sell it. And that is always the best reason for doing anything. Because I ask you to."

During my thirty-plus years in God's service, I've learned something very important. That is, from God's perspective, it's always about the people. Service to God is always about service to His people made in His image. He owns everything. We need to own nothing. And nothing but God should own us. Our loyalty is to God and to His Will for heaven and earth. While on earth we are managers, temporarily in charge of different aspects of His divine eternal Will. We are invited by Him to work together with Him to accomplish His purposes on earth. In this regard we are no different than the spirit beings who do the same in the unseen realm. Buildings come and go, wood rots, paint fades, metal rusts, fashions change. Yet opportunities are constantly provided for us to serve God by serving our fellow man. Everything on earth is temporary. His Will is eternal. He invites us to renounce the world of man's insatiable desires for pleasure and comfort, and to honor Him above all else, in the service of His Will. There is nothing better, nothing more rewarding.

Everything but God's Will is temporary, and if we are ignorant of this truth, we can be distracted by purchasing, owning, storing, and maintaining material things. If we become possessive of the materials He provides us with to accomplish His Will we can become entrapped in the preservation of 'things.' If we forget that nothing matters more than knowing and accomplishing God's Will, we become tied to the temporary, placing far too much value on material things which have no higher value other than to be used for accomplishing His Will.

It's been a long time since Michele and I met Chester and Betsy. August 1987 was a long time ago. None of us back then had any vision for what God had planned. None of us had seen the future; the Healing House Network, the Inn, or the hundreds of people who would come to the Inn from around the world by divine appointment. None of us in 1987 saw the thousands of lives that would be healed by the concepts and process of RTF as former ITC students returned to their home nations. Yet God saw all of it. He saw everyone. He saw the ones who would join us on this Misty Mountain. He knew them, called them by name, and directed them to Hendersonville. Some of them have been here a long time. Some left too early. Some slipped through the veil, their job finished, His Will accomplished. Some were born here, others died here. All were here by divine appointment. All had a role to play in a scene from Echo Mountain Inn. Everyone had a part to play in building the international network of RTF ministers. It's been a good ride, indeed! Thank you dear brothers and sisters!

Scene Three
Bobbing there on the surface of the sea, talking with God about EMI and the HHN, as I have been doing for more than fourteen years, I bowed my head humbly to my chest. Overcome with emotion, salty tears flowed from my closed eyes disappearing in the ocean. These were not tears of sorrow shed for the end of an era, but tears of gratitude for having been given the opportunity to serve God beside my brothers and sisters from around the world, through the RTF International Training Center at Echo Mountain Inn.

I prayed, "Thank You, Lord. I ask you to comfort Chester and Betsy as they take their bow and leave the stage as the primary leaders of RTF. And bless Lee and Cindy as they follow You, as You lead them into the next act of Your unfolding plan for RTF and the Healing House Network. I pray that You will continue to be glorified by our lives and by our service to Your children, our fellowman."

Misty Mountains

Mike Green
2004 ©

I exalt Your glory in these
misty mountains.
I embrace Your Presence
on this holy hill.
As Your radiance shines
through fragrant
evergreens,
I humbly offer You my will.

The fresh breeze of Your
Holy Spirit soothes me
As I kneel in secret in this
forest glen.
My heart sings with the
bluebird's gentle melody,
As Your tender love
enfolds me once again.

I praise You, O loving faithful Father!
In these misty mountains and on this holy hill;
I sing your praise, O gracious glorious Father!
As I humbly offer You my will.

I humbly offer You my will.

Bless God Ministries
mnmgreen@gmail.com

Chapter 15
Multiplying The Army

Yes, it is about His Will – and we knew that a big part of His Will for us was about the multiplication of what He had given to us. "Did you hear that?" "Did you see that?" we often whispered or texted to each other as we saw the Trainees "get it." Sometimes, these were profound, breathtaking moments.

It happened this way for one pastor couple. The leaders of their network had insisted they come for the entire five months of training. The man had been severely sexually abused as a small boy. Nearly 40 years later, the consequences of his victimization and wounding were spilling out over his leadership team and congregation. "Please help," his network leaders implored us. "This just can't continue."

We were planning to minister to him, probably during Training Module II. However, God got the jump on us during the Issue-Focused-Ministry practice in Module I. This man was teamed up with two young guys 20 years his junior. However, they had learned how to follow the IFM procedure, and so they did. They brought this hurting man to Jesus. As he poured out his rage, his devastation, and the total injustice of his abuse, the basement of his life was at last emptied. Gone were the resentment and defensiveness. "It wasn't your fault," the Lord told him. "You had nothing to do with this happening." The guilt and shame that had cloaked his life and made him unsafe for others were removed, gone. Gone for good. He was healed. It didn't take the Kylstras

56

to bring about this healing. It only took Jesus and the two young guys partnering with Him.

How many people's tears fell on that old green carpet in the dining room as this pastor courageously shared his poignant testimony? Our whole community rejoiced.

Every year in Training Module II, Trainers would teach on what to do when one's Ministry Receiver is not able to hear the Lord, when he is totally blocked. I clearly remember doing this teaching and encouraging the Trainees to just flow prophetically and chronologically. All of us, Trainers and Trainees alike, however, always hoped that our Ministry Receiver would be able to hear the Lord's voice, as this direct connection with God always brought the most healing.

One year, almost immediately after I had done this teaching, it happened while I was training Kate Featherstone. Her Ministry Receiver was incredibly damaged. She wept with frustration at her failure to hear the Lord. "Oh no," I thought silently, "can Kate's faith arise to prophetically pray for this lady?" I felt some tenseness going into the Soul/Spirit Hurts ministry, but gave Kate the go-ahead, knowing she had paid attention to the teaching. Kate launched out, prophetically lifting this woman's hurts to the Lord. The room was charged with God's Presence. Gradually the anguish on the woman's face melted as Jesus brought healing to her wounds. It was one of the most beautiful healings I have ever witnessed. Kate's confidence that the Holy Spirit would indeed be there for her rose about ten levels. God was multiplying the army so that the Kylstras were not needed.

Over and over again we were to see the power of the Holy Spirit working with our inexperienced Trainees, bringing amazing healing and freedom to their receivers. This truly inspired us to "keep going."

Tom and Pam Devitt, and Gary and Danise Duda; Ray and Emily Duenke, and Barry and Sandra Falkenstine; Mike and Michele Green, and John and Leslie Kindler; David and Linda Roeder, and Rodney and Kathy Tolleson.

Chapter 16
Steel Girders

Since the launch of the RTF Healing House Network in 2001, a number of amazingly capable people had brought their anointing and strength to further the RTF vision. They were the initial Steel Girders. Our "Seasoned Generals" included the Devitts, Dudas, Duenkes, Falkenstines, Greens, Kindlers, Roeders and Tollesons. Each of these outstanding ministry teams helped launch RTF. Because of them, RTF quickly gained a reputation as a safe place to receive ministry that was truly life changing.[1]

Change
In 2008 we felt a change coming. It was "in the air." It was also in the 'prayer.' Since our earliest days in ministry, we had received prophetic words about being "reproducers of reproducers of reproducers." It was going to take a large army to bring healing to the Bride of Christ. That army was going to need a lot of leaders. "God, send us those who can quickly move into places of leadership," we cried out. "We need them yesterday. The world seems to be knocking on our door." We knew we needed to be strong internally before opening the door too widely to receive the world. We knew we were not quite ready. "World, wait a minute. We still need a few more generals!"

---

[1] Others who played a significant role in the years before the Training Center were Lois Blanchard Bently, Tommy and Pat James, Steve and Cindy Bishop, Phil and Gloria Prather, Dorathy and Crawford Railey, Bob and Sue Thiede, and Gary and Susan Hedman. They were our faithful core team during the mid and late '90s.

New Leaders

Over the next several years, God answered our cries for leaders. We watched as they came; leaders such as the Guiers, Kellys, Bests, and a little later, the Samuels. These dedicated people were not necessarily more gifted than others in the network, but they generously made themselves available to work directly with us much of the year, which made the difference.

Bob and Cheria Guier, John and Erna Kelly, Mike and Phyllis Best, and David and Marilyn Samuels.

The Guiers would eventually oversee training at the International Training Center. The Kellys were just right to mobilize and focus prayer and intercession for the network. The Bests, with their organizational and people skills, helped us all grow as leaders. The Samuels, as ministry developers, proved to be just the right ones to connect RTF to other networks.

The Buckwheat's mission hearts took them to many places overseas, as they sacrificed to spread the RTF revelation.

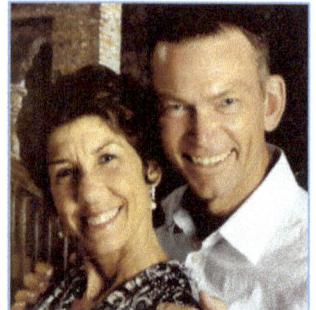

As new leaders brought their strengths to add to our strengths, more girders were erected. Later, other leaders, such as the Cowarts, Hulls, and Soares, would strengthen and lead regions.

Walter and Ida Cowart, George and Laurie Hull, and Herb and Cindy Soares.

Other HHN members made significant contributions, including many from other nations. They were RTF salt and light in their churches and in their regions – day in, day out. God used them to bring healing to His Bride.

For several years, as the new leaders were developing at EMI, we felt it tremendously important to connect them with the Seasoned Generals who came to faithfully pray and impart into them. We were almost ready to say, "Welcome World," but not quite. A few more Steel Girders needed to come into place.

Intercession
One primary internal strength we had as a network was powerful intercessors. Today, that still holds true. Beginning with Jeannie Mack, who moved here with us from Florida, others begin to join. We added Polly Altman, Jean Clark, Amy Martin, Sandra Falkenstein, Donna Compton, Sarada Sherrod, Ramona Barbara Volkots, and many more. Perhaps it was our greatest blessing that our ranks were filled with those who both loved prayer and prayed in an earnest and mature way. Steel Girders of prayer. What a difference each one of them made. Soon, we also discovered Sally Boenau who lived in our area. She became a valuable staff member and 'gatekeeper,' praying often at the front desk.

As John and Erna Kelly became the spear point for prayer, they mobilized and coordinated intercessory prayer efforts. The Kellys

vision was 24/7 prayer, in the sense that when one of us had a need, they could broadcast that alert to the entire intercessory network scattered around the world. At any given hour, someone somewhere could receive the email and begin praying. Although John has already gone to his heavenly home, Erna is faithful to continue this ministry even today with the help of the Winston and Pat Harveys. Myriads of prayers have been answered.

Resources

Although still needing refinement, our teaching and training resources were quite useable. They provided the guidelines for consistent reproduction of quality, proficient RTF ministers. Another Steel Girder was in place, but it would be strengthened further still in the future.

A bit of history: Our dear Jeannie Mack had headed up our Resource Department for many years when the ministry was based in Florida. In those days, we printed each RTF book in our own office. She prayed for each one that went out. Sadly we lost Jeannie to cancer in March, 2011. For us personally, it was a very big loss. During her illness, Maarten van der Muelen faithfully helped out for several years.

The Lord inspired the Mark and Julie Buckman to join us in Hendersonville to be trained in RTF ministry. We did not know at that time that Mark, an innovator and refiner, would one day head up our small but very vital Resource Department. Mark, along with his family, have become family and friends, as well as being RTF Healing House Network members.

Merry Christmas from the Buckmans

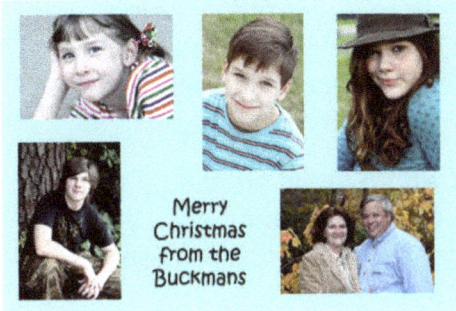

As I think about Mark and our care for him, a memory comes to my mind of the night that he unexpectedly went to the hospital and was told he needed emergency surgery. When Julie texted us this news, we immediately interrupted the conference we were leading and asked everyone to join us in prayer for him. We were thankful that he made such a good recovery.

Mark had a vision for what Resources could become. He was just right for this position. He was able to work with details, anticipate future needs, and implement the steps to get there. One example of where these giftings really paid off was the creation of the Observation Course for Step 1 of Training Module II. Mark videoed and edited this course. He then established it as an online training course. Further, based on my work as well as Bob Guier's, he pulled together the Training Manual to go with the course. No small job!

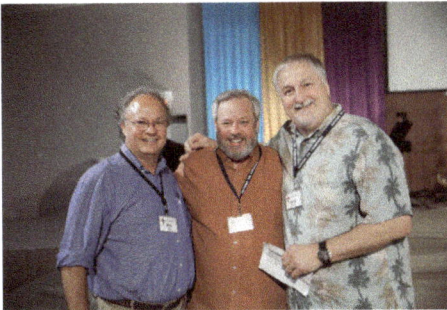

As an extrovert, Mark's friendliness on the phone and ability to communicate well have been a great asset. People report feeling his interest and support as they interact with him. Mark has a gift for making things fun.

In the past several years, Mark's gifting and loyalty have been greatly called upon. Under the Whitman's guidance, we are changing form and format of the delivery of many resources.

Mark's strengths and his willingness to serve at this crucial time are paramount as he helps carry RTF into the future. Mark has been a gift to this ministry, a behind-the-scenes Steel Girder.

Staff

Another source of Steel Girder strength lay in additional staff members the Lord brought to us. We share about our staff both in the chapter on "Behind The Scenes," and in "She Cleans Up Good," on pages 75 and 97.

God had given us emerging leaders, prayer strength, resources, and an excellent staff. There were many outstanding RTF ministers throughout the USA and in other parts of the world that were part of the network. We knew God was putting in place the Steel Girders that we needed to move ahead. We were getting closer to being ready to welcome the World.

Chapter 17
Acceleration, Expansion, Explosion

God had His plan for taking RTF to the world. During the years 2004 to 2015, He primarily took us to the world by having the world come to us. Don't you love how He surprises us in how He fulfills His prophetic word?

First, God sent people to the Inn to be trained who had an intense desire to take Restoring The Foundations back to their own countries. They reproduced RTF by training others, and we then went to their nations to undergird them. Agnieszka Rutkowska Wieja, her sister Asia, and her mom Anna, took RTF back to Poland. Andreas and Susanne Vogel likewise raised up others in Switzerland and Germany. Murray and Heather McCall saw that RTF was reproduced in New Zealand. Marcello and Jaque Orsi returned to Brazil and provided personal ministry and led the Healing and Deliverance seminar. Pieter and Elyse Van der Venter took RTF to South Africa including training new teams. George and Laurie Hull headed up the Canadian RTF network. Pastor David Lee, with the help of Deborah Ng, excitedly started RTF training in Singapore. Tom and Pam Devitt followed us to the UK as RTF missionaries, directing the first UK program. They later passed the UK directorship to Peter and Caroline Anderson. What had once been a "mom and pop" ministry was spreading its wings to touch the world.

Agnieszka Rutkowska Wieja, Asia Rutkowska, and Anna Rutkowska; Andreas and Susanne Vogel, and Murray and Heather McCall; Marcello and Jaque Orsi, and Pieter and Elyse Van der Venter; David Lee, Deborah Ng, and Peter and Caroline Anderson.

Secondly, the Lord accelerated the expansion by having the leaders of several major networks refer their own leaders to RTF for ministry and training. What an honor to minister to these "leaders of leaders," as well as to equip them to bring RTF into their networks.

John and Carol Arnott, who hosted a major revival in Toronto, influenced many leaders from around the world to receive a week of RTF healing ministry.

Thirdly, we have a network full of people with missionary hearts. Perhaps this started with us. When we attended Bible College in the 1980s, we thought we were preparing for the mission field. As it has turned out, we have actually traveled to many nations, but always on a temporary basis. Over the years, so many of us have sown RTF into foreign soil.

There have been more trips by more ministry teams than we can mention. Here are a few that you might find interesting. The Cowarts have reproduced in Mexico. One significant couple, Dennis and Diane Unrau, have served there for many years and become HHN members. The Briggs have made many trips to Asia and Poland. The Scheminskes have served on the mission field in Guatamala and Belize. The Barrys travel extensively in Asia. The Hanleys have sown in Ireland and Israel. The Bopps, along with teams from their church, have raised IFM teams in the

UK and Cameroon. The Falkenstines have given much to see Jamaicans raised up. The Choos have led Singaporean teams into surrounding Asian nations. The Ian Smiths trained a group of Nepalese people. The Brisbins led a team to Uganda to train IFM and Though Format teams. More recently, Donna Jollay, Brawers, Jeff and Sue Mead Stath, have begun to plant in Israel. The Banses frequently lead Iris teams into Israel to pray and serve. As of this writing, the Hazels are moving home to Saint Martin, excited about bringing RTF into the islands. And so goes the expansion of RTF to the world.

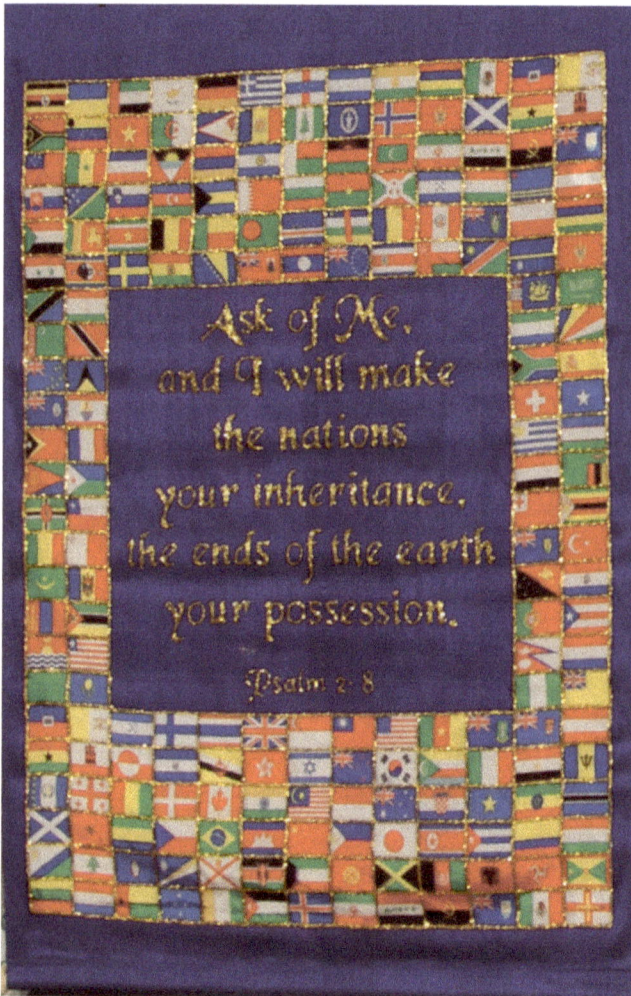

Ask of Me,
and I will make
the nations
your inheritance,
the ends of the earth
your possession.

Psalm 2: 8

Ira and Gloria Brawer, and John and Barbara Briggs; Win and Margaret Brisbin, and Judah and Hephzibab Choo; PJ and Kathy Hanley, and Rafael and Veronica Hazel; Donna Jollay, and Ian and Carissa Smith.

Being invited to touch nations can be an exhilarating, enticing thing if one is prepared. Or, it can be an extremely daunting thing if one is not. Chester and I knew that a few more final pieces needed to come into place before we were completely ready to say, "Welcome World, come and join us!"

SPECIAL MOMENTS – SPECIAL PEOPLE

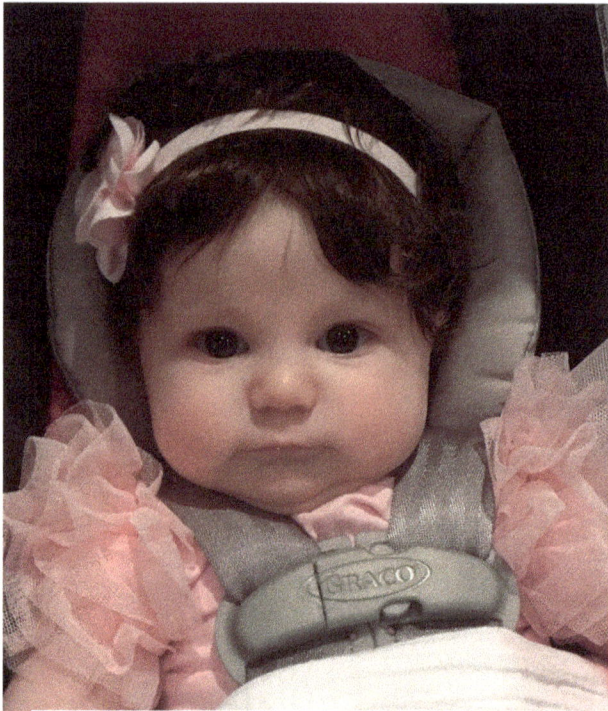

We believe in Miracles. Amira Blaze Graham born February 21, 2017, to Jeremey and Rebecca.

Chapter 18
Final Pieces

Exciting!

Great growth and expansion were taking place on all levels. Even though we had known it was coming, it still felt like being on a merry-go-round watching the scenery constantly change. Nothing stood still. "Can you believe how fast the ministry is growing?" we asked each other.

The Healing House Network, which started in 2001 with 25 people, had grown to over 200. A dozen or more ministry networks were referring their people to the RTF Healing House Network ministry teams for a week of ministry. The number of Trainees coming to the ITC was increasing, as well as those being trained elsewhere.

Chester and I saw that our greatest need was to put systems in place that would help ensure standardization and accountability; systems that would undergird stability; systems that would work at home as well as abroad.

Often, we found ourselves working far into the night hours as we developed and refined these systems. We would encourage each other with, "Have some tea, Love. If we stay up any later we may need some ice cream as a reward!" We so wanted each Ministry Receiver in any given nation to be assured of having the same quality of ministry and the same ingredients of ministry he would receive right here at the International Training Center. "It has to work just as well in Nepal and Cameroon as here," we both agreed. We have to provide universal standards.

Goals

Needless to say, between 2004-2014, we drank a lot of tea and ate too much ice cream! As we developed the needed systems to meet our goals, the final pieces began to come into place. Here is a summary of the main goals, with much appreciation to those who helped carry the load.

Goal 1) Improve Training Materials
- Update and create more user-friendly Issue-Focused Ministry publications and Ministry Tools manual. (Bob Guier, Michele Green, and others. Chester Kylstra: final editor)

Goal 2) Standardize World-Wide Systemic Training
- Create Video Course for the Observation Step of the Through Format Training. This cornerstone resource will ensure that all English speaking Trainees are exposed to the same basic principles and applications of the RTF ministry revelation. (Betsy Kylstra, Bob Guier, and Mark Buckman)
- Develop Guidelines and Evaluations for Trainers (Betsy Kylstra and Bob Guier)

Goal 3) Clarify HHN Benefits, Expectations, and Responsibilities
- Create Policies and Procedures Manual (Chester Kylstra and Brenda Mabus)
- Update Plans & Procedures for Healing House Network members (Chester and Betsy Kylstra, Bob and Cheria Guier, and many HHN ministry teams)

Goal 4) Protect/Safeguard Ministers as well as Ministry Receivers
- Use Character Evaluation approach developed by Bishop Bill Hamon's 10 M's.[1] (Starting with Thorough Format Training)

---

[1] The "10 M's" have been used for many years by Bill Hamon and Christian International ministers. He finally published these

Goal 5) Ensure Successful Training at Training Center

- Screen and evaluate potential Trainees. Make sure those coming for training are actually capable of successfully receiving training. (Chester and Betsy Kylstra, Susan Rhodes, and Brenda Mabus)

Goal 6) Promote Network Connectedness

- Establish a world-wide Intercessory Prayer capability network to share needs for united prayer. (John and Erna Kelly, later assisted by Winston and Pat Harvey)
- Establish USA "In-Touch" communication with each HHN member. A monthly contact by network chaplains. (Mike and Phyllis Best, followed by Dick and Joan Bowen)

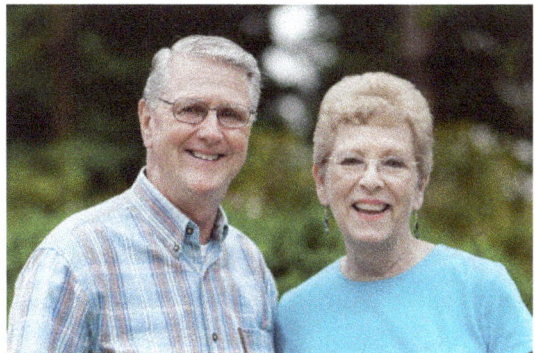

These systems made up the final needed Steel Girders. Now RTF could support whatever weight was put upon it. Now as the world knocked on our door, we would have the courage to say, "Ok World, we are ready. Come on in!" Weary but content, we breathed a sigh of relief. "Have some ice cream, dear."

---

evaluation principles in his book, *How Can These Things Be? A Preacher and a Miracle Worker but Denied Heaven!*, June 15, 2015.

SPECIAL MOMENTS – SPECIAL PEOPLE

In recent years (2014-2017) we have had the opportunity to train a number of awesome younger people who became Healing House Network members. Thank you David and Marilyn Samuels for pioneering the relationship with YWAM and helping to build with IRIS Ministries. A number of these people are:

Karen Bensler
Mary Bernal
Chelsea Bouma
Ashley Brewer
Peter Choi
Vinnie DeMarco
Jessica Daniel Espinera
Jason Ghist

Chirs Hartwick
Khanh Ho
Matilda Loof
Diana Neville
Ian and Hilde Norheim
Megan Shipman
Cindy Simpson
Ian & Carissa Smith
Gillian Thompson

RTF team train IRIS Harvest School students in Johannesburg, South Africa.

Chapter 19
Behind The Scenes

Behind every successful man is a good woman, and certainly, behind our growing and successful ministry was an incredibly faithful and talented staff. They worked at the front desk, in the kitchen, in the guest rooms, on the grounds, in resources, or in the administration building. Although they were mostly hidden from sight, our staff was central to everything that took place at the Inn, Training Center, and Healing House Network.

Susan Rhodes was the pleasant voice that an inquiring Ministry Receiver usually heard on the phone. Listening with discernment and speaking with wisdom, she has provided comfort, perspective, and prayer to many a hurting heart. What a God-send she has been. If it were not for confidentiality, Susan could write an unbelievable book about Ministry Receivers' calls! If you were to ask her, she might tell you about some of the more wild communications she has received, such as the request from an African man to house his goats while he was here for training. Susan's sense of humor has brought much needed levity on many a stressful day, and her personal faith has always been an inspiration. Enjoy reading Susan's personal account of her time with RTF at the end of this chapter.

Brenda Mabus couldn't have come to us at a better time. Greatly needed was her willingness to serve and her administrative/ organizational gifts. She helped Chester develop guidelines for the HHN, typed and refined numerous documents, and was key in pulling off conferences. Brenda is a skilled Anticipator.' She was usually a job or two ahead, planning for things three or four months out. Her office was bathed with life-giving IHOP music. Brenda delighted at being "Aunt Brenda" for the Fortier's precious little girl Eliana.

Did Brenda and Susan make a powerful working combination? You bet! Susan and Brenda worked together solving RTF HHN problems, screening potential Trainees, and gathering the many Ministry Receivers needed for Module III. One training season, we needed 120 Ministry Receivers! You know how much work it takes to make arrangements for just one person! With God's grace, they found everyone needed. We heavily depended on Brenda and Susan, on their love for the Lord, and on their deep desire to see RTF move forward.

Sherry Douglas and I occupied the middle room in the Admin building across from Brenda and Susan. Sherry, who had been the head counselor at another ministry for many years, who had had her own administrative assistant, miraculously agreed to be my assistant! "I will help you as long as you need me," she told me many times. What a difference her wisdom, prayers and friendship have made to me personally and to the effectiveness of my ministry position.

Together we answered the majority of emails that came to the ministry. "Sherry," I would say, feeling stressed, "if we say it 'this way,' they will be angry and upset. If we put it 'this other way,' they will

probably be offended. How shall we try to 'put it?' I really don't want to jump into a swamp of alligators, if we can help it." Sherry would be quiet for a minute and then out would pop her suggestion.

So often when I heard her solution, I knew it was "just right." It would be full of grace, but also to the point. "Now, how did she do that?" I would wonder. We made a great team!

Sherry and I had a world map. Together we watched and rejoiced as the fingers of RTF stretched out and touched more and more nations. "Wow! Look at that," one of us would exclaim.

Stephanie Fortier managed the Inn's front desk and also did the accounting for the Inn and the ministry. Stephanie was accurate, diligent, and faithful. She had both the overview skills and the ability to work with many details. She could be counted on for excellence.

Chester oversaw both Brenda and Stephanie. The three of them had almost identical Kendell Life Language profiles, which illustrated why they worked together easily and harmoniously.

You can see why we looked forward to our time in the office with this amazing team. They were a special gift to us during the important years of rapid expansion. We cherish their contributions to us and to RTF.

And here is Susan's warm and engaging account of her time at Echo Mountain Inn. Enjoy!

Susan's Story
Susan Rhodes

Living in Hendersonville since 1980, I knew Echo Mountain Inn existed but had never spent much time there. I did visit the Inn one time when the restaurant was in operation. Later, my husband, Richard and I (we married in 1984), had dinner several times at the Inn. In fact, we attended a Christmas party one year. Little did I know that one day, God would bring me to Echo Mountain Inn to begin ministry training and to eventually work there.

On Christmas Eve, 2003, the Kylstras attended the service at our church. I had written, *"Christmas from the Heart,"* a Christmas worship experience which was God-inspired and included our choir, praise team, band, and the youth and children. After the service, my husband came up to me and introduced me to Betsy and Chester Kylstra, who had been sitting behind him. They told me who they were and shared briefly about their ministry. My heart leaped as Betsy was sharing. She gave me a book. Immediately I knew this was the ministry I wanted to be involved in. They mentioned that they were buying the Echo Mountain Inn as a public Bed and Breakfast, but also it was their dream to house a training center for the ministry, Restoring The Foundations.

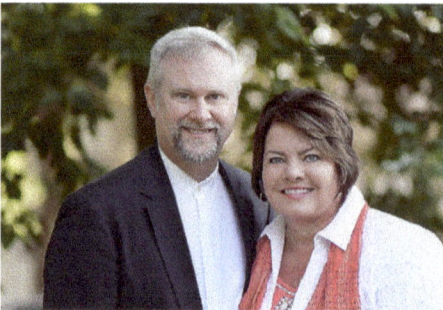

In the early part of 2004, the Kylstras were in the midst of purchasing the Inn. Their plan was to accomplish the needed renovation and then begin the first training class in August. They invited us up to the Inn to pray and to help them with important contacts in the community. Richard was a good resource for them as he has lived in

Henderson County his entire life. He was able to answer many questions about the area.

I remember meeting on the sunporch at the Inn. What a lovely place with a view of the town of Hendersonville nestled in the mountains of the Blue Ridge. As I stood on the sunporch this scripture from Psalm 121 came to mind: *"I will lift up my eyes to the hills—From whence comes my help? My help comes from the Lord, Who made heaven and earth."*

I began my Issue-Focused Ministry training, along with my friend Jodie Nolf, the winter of 2005. One week, a terrible snow storm was forecast to arrive in the evening. We were advised to stay at the Inn rather than trying to drive down the mountain that evening and back up the next morning. I only lived 14 minutes away, but staying at the Inn was the better and safer idea.

It turned out to be a special evening and night. I have such a wonderful memory of the cozy double room we stayed in, the Sage Room. It was a beautiful sage green with comforting quilts on the beds and a quaint little sitting area. I do remember the thin walls and hearing conversation from the next room. It was close quarters, just like family.

As the year progressed, I was praying for a job opportunity. One day Betsy called me "out of the blue" and offered me a part-time position at the Inn's front desk. I was thrilled. This was just what I had been praying for. I started as a front desk clerk in August 2005, the same month that Greg and Stephanie Fortier came as the new Innkeepers. We learned "the ropes" together, from making reservations to learning the accounting software.

I enjoyed working at the front desk and greeting our guests. Some were local while others were from all parts of the world. One of my favorite things in the spring and summer was to leave the front door open to feel the cool breeze, to hear the nearby water fountain, and to listen to the birds sing. So many different varieties; all singing their distinct song, sort of like our guests, I suppose.

In October, 2006, Betsy and Chester asked me if I would leave the front desk position and come work in the ministry office. "Of course," I said. I was excited to serve RTF as it was helping so many people.

I started as the RTF Healing House Network Ministry Coordinator. I moved across the driveway to the Administration Building. When training started in the winter I helped with the new Trainees to ensure they had what they needed as they prepared to come for training.

What stories I could tell. Such an array of questions. They came by phone calls and emails. They ranged from, "Which airport was closest?" to, "What type clothing and underwear to bring." One year we had a fellow from Africa apply for training. He wanted to know where he could keep his goats. I didn't bat an eye. I responded back to him that the Echo Mountain Inn is a "pet free, animal free facility." We still chuckle about that one.

Sometimes the phone calls that come in are difficult ones. They are from hurting people who want to be heard and want to be healed. While I can 'hear' their hearts, and encourage them, it is when they go through the RTF ministry that they are really helped. Some make it a point to come meet me. They almost always say, "Thank you for matching me up with just the right ministry team. I am a changed person. I can now move forward in what God has called me to." Then it is all worthwhile.

At times, we did have some animals roaming the property, even though the Inn has a "pet free" policy. Animals in their natural habitat frequently "came by." We have spotted wild turkeys, and an occasional deer or bear. Then there is the groundhog we named "Hank." The most common animal is the squirrel. They created hiding places within the walls of the Admin Building as well as the ministry rooms. In one ministry room, a squirrel dug his way through the wall and stuck his head out from behind a wall tapestry. What a big surprise for the ministry team. That hole was quickly spackled and repaired. Since then, that ministry room has been lovingly called the "Squirrel Room."

On any given day, you can see squirrels playing all around the Inn and grounds. They like to walk the power lines behind the Admin Building and ministry rooms. On several occasions, while in one of the ministry rooms, I've seen a squirrel peering in the window. I have to chuckle because it reminds me of a story about a preacher who was giving a Children's Sermon one Sunday. He asks the children, "Can you tell me what is gray, furry, has a bushy tail and eats nuts?" A little boy replies, "Preacher, it sounds to me like a squirrel but I know the answer has to be Jesus." Now every time I see a squirrel while doing ministry, no matter what is going on, I'm reminded, I know the answer is "Jesus." What a way to keep focused on Him!

I remember once a week gathering in the "upper room" in the ministry building for staff prayer. This would include personal prayer needs, prayers for the leadership, prayers for the ministry locally and internationally, and prayers for the Inn. This was a special time of bonding with each other and really caring about one another's needs.

I truly loved being asked to lead worship during ministry training or for a special event. It seemed that it didn't take long for everyone to be in one accord and enter into worship. We could feel the tangible Presence of the Lord.

There is something very special about the Inn and it will always hold a special place in my heart.

I've experienced "life's changing seasons" during my 12 years working here. I've made some dear, lifelong friends; had some health challenges; grieved the deaths of friends, family members and the loss of staff members; celebrated weddings, births and adoptions; gone through a change in leadership; had "mountain top experiences" with God, and I have a few more wrinkles.

I've enjoyed all the different seasons at the Inn. The fall is the peak season, when guests come to visit and view the beautiful fall colors. Winters are beautiful as well when the snow started falling and all that can be heard is a quiet calmness. The Inn is always decorated for Christmas with several trees and lights inside and out. Of course, spring and summer bring forth the many flowers blooming on the property; the daffodils, azaleas, daisies, tiger lilies and my very favorite, the hydrangeas.

We have some stately pine trees and beautiful hemlocks that provide a comforting blanket. One in particular supports a swing that youngsters love to play on. It was so sad a few years back, when several majestic trees had to be taken down because of disease.

Echo Mountain Inn is a tranquil place. Recently, as I was walking the peaceful grounds of the Inn, I asked the Lord, "Why does this place feel so familiar to me?" I felt prompted to look at the rock foundation. Then it dawned on me. The house that my granddaddy built in Madison County had a very similar stone foundation. I would guess that the rock is some type of granite used in the late 1800s and early 1900s. It is probably native to Western North Carolina. How fitting that the physical foundations of the two buildings have this commonality. Both impacted my foundation. Except my foundation was restored at Echo Mountain Inn. I'm very grateful for the years I've spent here in work and in ministry. "Thank you, Betsy and Chester."

Chapter 20
Our Grand Old Lady Has Class

Our Grand Old Lady, our chosen Inn, just loved to host celebrations for people of all ages.[1] That's when she was at her best. With her big picture windows and colorful sun-porch, she provided a relaxed, comfortable atmosphere for family reunions and informal parties. She also loved to get decked out and host an elegant bash for an intimate wedding reception. With white tablecloths and candlelight, romance danced in every corner. The very next day, when her white table cloths were sent to the cleaners, and the last wedding cake crumbs swept away, she could make herself just right for a children's birthday party. With Maarten van der Muelen twisting red and yellow animal balloon figures and doing tricks, children's happy giggles would fill her dining room and drift out to her lawn. No white tablecloths and candlelight now, just lots of big gooey ingredients to make ice

---

[1] Our Grand Old Lady, otherwise known as Echo Mountain Inn, has been hosting people since the 1920s. If you would like to learn more about her history, you may do so in Appendix A on page 143.

cream sundaes. Oh boy! Versatility was our Grand Old Lady's middle name. She thrived on it.

At times, she stretched out her big arms to the larger community. She hummed to herself as several hundred people with the Tour of Historic Inns loitered in her lovely rooms and "oohed" and "aahed" over her. "Come back soon," she beckoned to them.

On occasion, a new bride and groom would choose her Royal Room for their wedding night. "May your unity be blessed," she would whisper. There were also times when couples who had spent their honeymoon with her 25 or 50 years earlier would return for an anniversary night. "You didn't forget me," she would smile to herself, as they asked for their original rooms.

Always ready to provide the appropriate background for the richness of life to happen within her walls, our Grand Old Lady had a secret, a very big one.

Her secret was an amazing staff of creative people who pampered her hourly - day and night. For more than a decade, Greg and Stephanie Fortier were her primary "Keepers." They learned and displayed her history. They gave her vitamin pills for her aches and pains, and they were ever so patient with her old age irregularities. Having an eye for her period furnishings. they wanted her beautifully adorned for everyone to enjoy.

Coming from the Toronto Airport Christian Fellowship, the Fortiers were an excellent fit for the community here. Their vision was to run a retreat center for pastors and leaders to receive refreshing and healing. One might say that our match with them was hand in glove.

Was there anything Greg couldn't fix? He was in his element since something, usually more than one thing, ALWAYS needed fixing. Having a genuine gift of welcoming, he created a family atmosphere as different groups came. Greg's hospitality gifts sparkled in an endearing way during our Grand Old Lady's special events. His spirit of servanthood often caused the more mature women to adopt him in their hearts as a son or nephew.

Stephanie, with her flare for organization, made overseeing the front desk look as smooth as a freshly paved road. The front desk also served as a "crises center," where problems and emergencies were handled. Stephanie and her staff kept their cool in the midst of it all. She did a great job as the accounting manager for both the ministry and the Inn. Being the mother of a small child, she did a lot of juggling to make it work.

The staff working closely by the Fortier's sides included artistic Stuart Findlay, facilities manager; Sally Boeneau, 'gatekeeper' at the front desk; and Lydia Castanada, who prayed over each room as she cleaned them. We have also had several outstanding chefs through the years: Jen Eckart and Greg Kilpatrick, as well Kay Vazquez, who also cooks for her restaurant in Saluda, NC. These chefs cooked daily during our training modules. Oh how our Trainees complained about gaining weight at the same time they were going back for second helpings!

'Comradery' was the word, as the staff worked together to enhance our Grand Old Lady's atmosphere and purposes. It took many people to bring out her very best and allow her to be seen as the remarkable old lady that she is.[1] They did it.

---

[1] Please note that there were many others who came for a season and contributed their giftings to the Grand Old Lady and her Innkeeper. Some of those who worked with him were Jerry Barton, Tim Turner, Maarten van der Muelen, Joyce Wright. Kelly Fiveash, Kathy Layman, Jason Grist, and Ashlyn McGinnis.

SPECIAL MOMENTS – SPECIAL PEOPLE

David and Linda Roeder dancing to "Eagle's Wings."

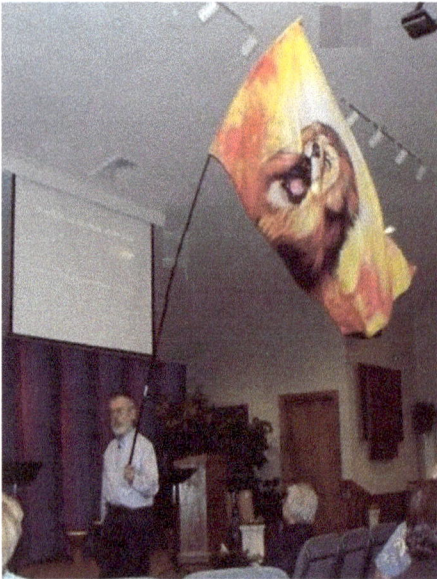

Chester with the
Lion of Judah flag.

Chester and Betsy
teaching in Singapore.

Chapter 21
Hidden Shifts

As life continued at the Inn, some shifts were gradually, subtly, but permanently taking place. These shifts were a good thing.

For 13 years, the Inn, or really what it represented, had been our vision. We had literally dreamed about it, spearheaded the financing to buy it, and substantially invested in it. Now at last, the Inn was actually owned by the ministry, and functioning as a place to encounter God. "Our vision" was happening.

This warm inviting place said to each one who gathered around us, "Come, you are welcome here. Come rest awhile and enjoy my views. Come pray awhile and be refreshed. Come laugh awhile and make new friends. Come worship awhile and draw nearer to God. Come work awhile and be trained to bring God's freedom." She would extend her welcome to each one as they ate in her cheerful dining room, viewed the Misty Mountains through one of her many windows, or chatted by her double fireplace.

Can you imagine the thrill and satisfaction we felt when our Healing House Network friends first gathered there? They filled up the dining room, slept in the bedrooms, walked around the lawn and swimming pool, or cozied down in the Sun Porch's wicker furniture. It was as if our family had come home.

There were so many of us. At one time, 110 people were hosted and fed during our Healing House Network days. The roar of voices was music to us. Worship, ascending right into the heavenlies, was a high point. We looked into the beautiful faces of our friends, and loved each one.

At some point we would leave the laughter and good conversations. Chester and I, from our nearby home, would watch as various lights in different bedrooms were shut off. We deeply felt the connectedness, the bonding of lives and hearts and purpose. We had that exhilarating sense of being the father and mother of a network.

The Shift

As our larger family came 'home,' the Inn, which once had only been our dream, now belonged to all of us. The RTF family had made what was once our vision their vision. It became a wonderful shared home.

As our RTF family grew to love the Inn, they wanted to help fix her up, to make her even more beautiful and comfortable. She became like a magnet for people's generosity. Those first few years were like Echo Mountain Inn Christmas. She beamed as people gave financial love gifts, adopted her rooms to care for, and added beautiful and appropriate furnishings to her and her surrounding buildings. Yes, one gave an antique pump organ; another, beautiful, handcrafted bookcases; and still another French lace curtains. Margi Wynn, a notable artist, delivered six beautiful original paintings. Yet another friend brought an antique wicker couch for the Sun Porch that matched my grandmother's wicker chairs.

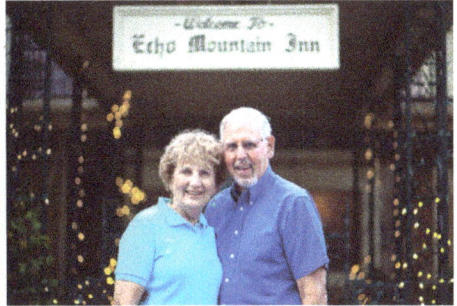

Don and Iris Valley – Antique Pump Organ, Phil and Margi Wynn – Paintings.

Then the Tollesons came for a week with ten skilled craftsmen in tow. They came to make drapes and valances, to lay tile, to correct the plumbing, and to set in a big Jacuzzi. They came to create a room ready for royalty.

Julie Buckman also lent her artistic abilities, along with Jeannie Mack, to create lovely updated bedrooms by making drapes bedspreads, and pillows. They changed white or beige to color.

Before and After: Julie and Jeannie brought life to many rooms.

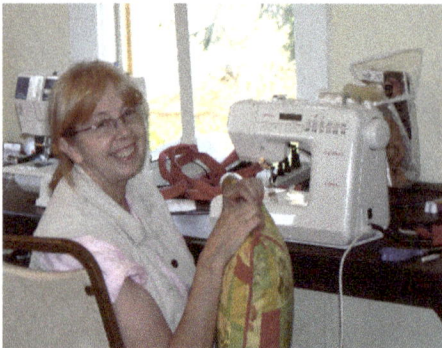

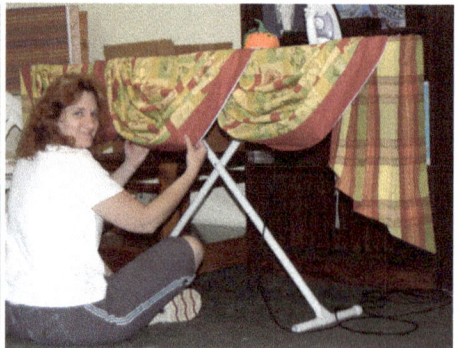

Jeannie was a gifted seamstress. Julie could work wonders. This talented combo brought beauty and style to the Grand Old Lady.

Walter and Ira Cowart brought their tool boxes from Washington State and greatly enhanced the pool area by building a bathhouse. Our Inn, which now belonged to us all, was vibrant with new life. It was almost as if our Grand Old Lady shared our vision rather than just housing it.

Another subtle shift: Can you imagine what else might be happening? Many of the Inn's guests had been coming for decades. One returning couple had had their honeymoon there fifty years ago. It was not uncommon to hear when they arrived in the foyer, "Oh my goodness. It seems so much lighter. Did you repaint this entire area?" "No, we haven't," we would reply. However, we knew that the very giver of Light resided here.

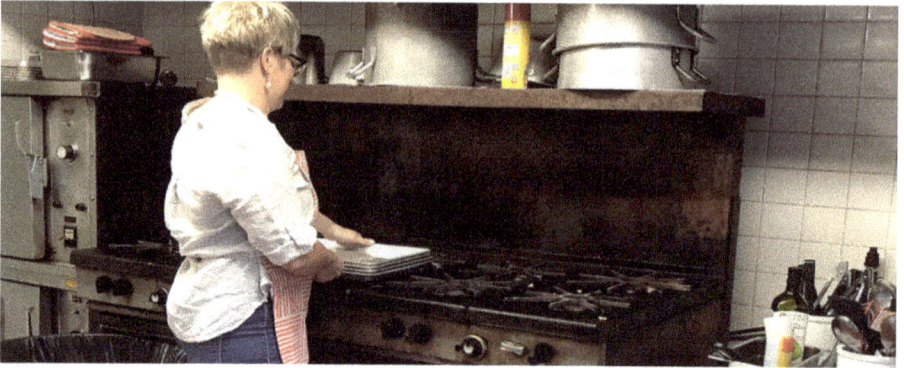

Chapter 22
Ladies: What To Do In A Crises

You know food is important, especially when people are working hard, are under stress, and need a relaxing and cheerful break. Our dream was that food at the Training Center would be both enjoyable and healthy. Chefs Martha and Jen got us off to a great start in the early years, setting a high standard. However, the time came when they were not able to continue.

"Let's plan ahead," Chester said to me, "and get our chef in place well in advance of the start of the winter training modules." "Great idea," I replied, "lets position ourselves for a smooth transition." Bravo for us. It is so good to be proactive. However, our great plan sounded better than it worked.

That June, we began to interview for our chef. We found a local man, who said he was eager to manage a restaurant at the Inn as well as working through the winter Training Modules. He seemed to be in agreement with our desire for quality food. We hired him.

Looking back, it would have been incredibility helpful if ten red flags had fallen out of the sky, shouting "No, No, No,", or, "Don't you dare," or, "What are you thinking?" In the absence of red flags, we proceeded.

The first red flag did appear soon after the man was hired. He wanted to purchase several deep fat fryers. Actually, he wanted to fry everything but the bread. "Oh no." Five months of deep fat fried food every day is just too much! This chef never quite forgave us for refusing his request. (By the way: Please don't do a restaurant unless you hear the audible voice of God saying it's your calling, and it's your only option!)

By December, our restaurant was still losing money. While Echo Mountain Inn had once been known for its fine dining, our chef was not able to get us close to that level of excellence. I'm sure our 'restaurant' was actually a bit of an insult to our Grand Old Lady's standards.

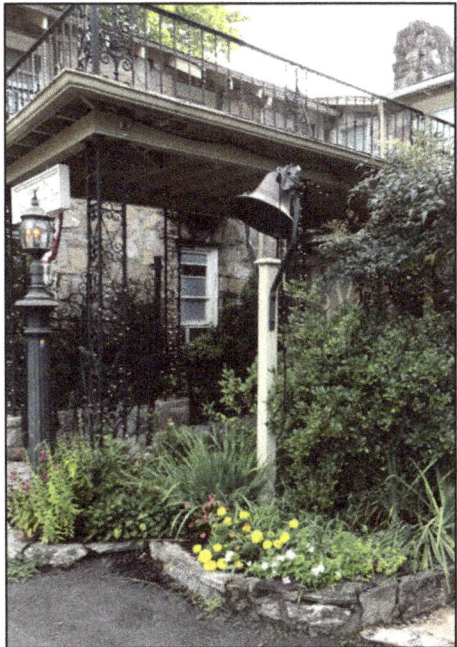

Early January came with its snow and high winds, and logs crackling in the double fireplace. In just six days, the Module I Trainees would be arriving. As we met with our chef, prepared to go over the next week's menus, he mockingly smiled and handed us his resignation. We couldn't believe it. How dare him! We had put up with his miserable, frustrating behavior for all of these months, and now he was quitting. Caught somewhere between relief and fury, we asked him to stay until the end of the week so he could train our new chef in EMI's kitchen. He agreed, looking at us with arrogance. It was obvious he thought we would never be able to find someone to replace him in that short length of time.

We both took a deep breath. It was one of those moments that challenged the popular saying, "When God closes one door, He opens another." We prayed, and we reminded each other that this was no surprise to Him. We agreed that He already had the solution to this problem, even if at that moment we had no clue what it was.

I had an appointment to get my hair done in just an hour. Crises or not, we agreed I was to keep the appointment. And herein is our prescription. Don't miss it, ladies.

> When all else fails, when it's just not working, go to the beauty salon and get your hair done.

Soon my head, covered in shampoo, was deep in the sink. Explaining our crisis, I asked my beautician, "Do you by chance know someone who might be able to cook for us?" Before she could answer, a shampoo-covered head rose up out of the sink to my right and said, "I've had a number of years' experience running a dining room for 300 people. Would I qualify? I am not working right now." "Absolutely perfect," I delightedly articulated through the soap bubbles. "Can you get started soon, like this afternoon?

Two hours later Chester and I and our new chef (whom we hoped could cook) walked into our commercial kitchen so she could begin her training. As we introduced her to the about-to-be previous chef, he looked as if he were seeing a ghost. Yet another of God's perfectly timed, divine coincidences.

So ladies, never pass up an opportunity to get your hair done, no matter what the crisis.

Samuels' Make-Over of the Front Desk.

Chapter 23
"She Cleans Up Real Good"

Many "moving forward" activities were taking place at our Inn, or within the shadow of her gates. She seemed pleased with our win-win relationship. She seemed to enjoy extending herself as she watched over the rich experiences happening within her walls. Greg, along with Stuart Finlay, spent countless hours behind the scenes repairing and updating her many systems, heading off emergencies. They were renowned for their abilities to come up with inexpensive solutions even when they faced great challenges.

There is an old saying that goes like this. "She cleans up real good." It may be poor English, but when it came to our Grand Old Lady it really fit. It was time again for another round of "powder and paint." By 2012, she was beginning to look bedraggled. Her makeup had worn a bit too thin.

Her downstairs public rooms, including her foyer, disparately needed a complete make-over. Dave and Marilyn Samuels were willing to take the reins, overseeing much of the challenging upgrade. "Listen in" as they share their adventure.

God's Provision
David Samuels

For over a decade the Echo Mountain Inn was lovingly run by a group of Christians whose goal was to create an environment where people could come and be healed, enjoy each other, and encounter God's peace in a profound way. Innkeepers, Greg and Stephanie Fortier, along with Betsy and Chester, founders of Restoring the Foundations Ministry, led a team of people with a variety of gifts and talents - all working together to keep this beautiful historical building running like a well oiled machine.

RTF is a ministry of excellence. And the Inn needed to reflect that excellence. People from all walks of life came to Echo Mountain Inn to receive ministry. And most importantly on their road to personal healing, to encounter a loving God. It was a struggle to balance the quest for excellence with the shoe-string budget that maintained the Inn but had little room for renovations.

After about a decade of continual use, the Inn was beginning to look 'tired.' "As hard as you scrub and as much as you work, you can never get a worn-out carpet to look totally clean." It was time for a facelift, but where was the money for one? We, along with many others, had a vision for what it could look like. On our own it was impossible to accomplish. Of course, that's when God made a way.

The real blessing of being a part of the facelift was to watch how God blessed each step of the process. Truly, it was a joy to see how God met each need as we dared to dream beyond what our shoestring budget could afford. As we moved from room to room in the public areas there were unique, supernatural ways He brought favor, blessings and provision to complete this amazing transformation.

A donor came forward with an idea. He offered to donate $5,000 in matching funds to encourage people to give. For every dollar donated, he would match that dollar, thus doubling the donation. Once the idea was expressed, another person was inspired put forth a second $5,000 to be matched. Before we knew it, we had raised $20,000 for the facelift!

The first problem was green. Green carpet, green paint on the walls, even the beams in the ceiling were painted - you guessed it - green! No one knew how old the carpet was, but it was definitely the cleanest old carpet the flooring contractor had ever seen. The big question was, "What's under the Green Carpet?" We were hoping for hardwood, and we weren't disappointed! As we ripped out the old carpet, we found beautiful hardwood floors wall-to-wall!

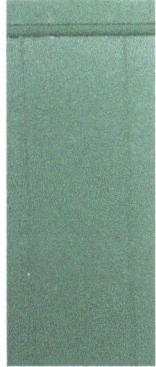

A woman who was staying at the Inn saw what we were doing. Even though she wasn't related to RTF, she donated the money needed to have the floors refinished! This was another example of how God moved in miraculous ways to see our vision of the 'make-over' accomplished.

We had the floors refinished to a new shine and then we got working on the green paint. Swatches were consulted and various squares of sample paint were splashed on the wall for review. In the end we chose a neutral beige to cover the green, a wonderful color that would

Winston and Pat Harvey found many ways to help improve EMI.

not clash with any bride's color scheme. A special thanks to Greg, Stuart and Jerry, Sally, the Harveys, RTF students and RTF family members who worked tirelessly to see the job done.

Next we took on the decor. Many of the previous furnishings and furniture had been found at Good Will or Habitat for Humanity. Some of them were worn out before they came to us. After 10 more years of use, they were ready to be changed.

Marilyn is an amazing interior designer. She has a knack for color coordination, decorations, and is also highly favored by

God to get great buys. After weeks of scrounging used furniture stores and outlets, we finally found an Estate Silent Auction store that had some amazing furniture, lamps, and other items that were very high quality and in great shape. The problem was, we had to 'bid' on them.

In a silent auction, if you like a piece, you fill out a slip of paper that has a place for you to put a dollar amount. This is the bid you make for the item. You hope it is the highest bid they receive, because that's the only way you win the item. It would appear that God wanted the beautiful furniture to go to the Inn, because we just happened to run into an employee of the store as he was leaving. We asked him, "What is the best strategy to use to win an item?" He gave us an unexpected answer.

He told us that instead of putting a dollar amount on the bid line, we could just write the words, "Highest bid plus $5." "If we did that," he assured us, "you will win every item on which you bid."

That's exactly what we did. Can you believe we came back with two beautiful couches, two wing back chairs, a lamp and several other items? We paid so little for the items that we still had money left over to do more shopping.

To our amazement, we found some hanging tiffany lights for which we paid $15 each. Later we turned them into beautiful table lamps by salvaging stands from other used lamps. Next we found beautiful credenzas and hutches that had scratches on the tops. We bought these for pennies on the dollar. We were able to either finish these ourselves, or put a nice runner over the scratched areas. Things were beginning to take shape for the Inn.

Another miraculous find had to do with the front desk foyer. The registration desk had been put together piecemeal with a tired counter and mismatched desks. It did not give the best "first impression." It was definitely time for something new. We found a store that installed custom granite tops in homes and businesses. They had several unbelievably beautiful "remnant pieces" that we could use as a new front desk counter as well as a coffee bar top in the dining room. We paid very little for these "left over" pieces that just "happened" to fit our needs. We were so inspired that we replaced cabinets and installed new lighting to complete our vision for a new foyer.

Marilyn focused on setting an atmosphere of comfort and style with attention to details like silk flowers, matching frames with prints, knick-knacks, area rugs, lamps, pictures and odds and ends. With the Lord's help, she took the ordinary and made it extraordinary! With her eye for colors, traffic patterns and flare to make the decorations flow from one room to another, she took a beautifully updated space and turned it into a gorgeous quintessential Inn that represented the excellence of Restoring the Foundations ministry.

101

The last step in revamping the Inn was to repave the cracked and pot holed driveway and parking lot. It had reached the "Drive at your own risk" stage. Just in time, the Lord brought in two donors who put forward the $50,000 needed to finish the job.

We are so thankful to all those who helped with the hours of painting, scraping, pulling nails, fixing toilets, and moving furniture back and forth until it was positioned "just right". But mostly, we are thankful to the Lord for blessing the work of all the hands who helped with this renovation, and for giving us this wonderful haven in the mountains, a place of rest, peace and healing. The beautifully renovated Inn had become once again a place where people could get away for a season of refreshing and encounter a loving God, who came to bring them Abundant Life.

(Continue Kylstras…) What a joy it was, to watch the Inn becoming more beautiful day by day.

My mother always used the words "quite remarkable" to describe any elderly woman who somehow managed to pull it all together and look a bit elegant. "Well there is Miss Hattie Smith," she would say. "She looks quite remarkable, now, doesn't she?" The good news was that after her "Samuels make over," our Grand Old Lady, at well over 100 years old, now qualified – she looked the part. She is "quite remarkable," I thought, so proud of her new appearance.

SPECIAL MOMENTS – SPECIAL PEOPLE

Betsy Kylstra demonstrating how to achieve a score of 5.0 on the RTF Thorough Format Ministry Evaluation!

SPECIAL MOMENTS – SPECIAL PEOPLE

Several Graduating Classes

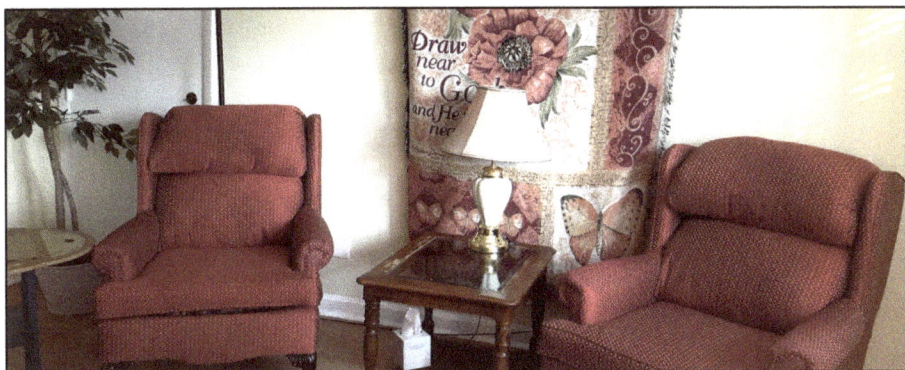

Chapter 24
Worth It?

We had so many God touches, so many faith-filled experiences per square inch of our lives that sometimes I thought I would pop right out of my skin – or be translated into eternity. These were unforgettable days, even seasons, when the word 'blessing' just wasn't rich enough to sum it up.

There were also a few times, however, when we felt exhausted, stretched to the limits, and weary with having so little discretionary time. Amidst the cloud of discouragement, we would searchingly ask ourselves, "Is it worth it?" That soul-searching question, rather than driving us to despair, was most often a catalyst in connecting us once again with our deep passion to see people healed, to raise up an army, and to provide a place for God Encounters.

From the beginning, the Inn proved to be a very safe environment for both the training and also for the personal ministry that took place throughout the year. Week after week, people came from around the USA as well as from other nations. Some referred to this week of healing prayer as a 'class' or 'course.' Others called it 'counseling.' Still others spoke in hushed tones of "my deliverance week."

Whatever people called it, the large majority of them were met by the Lord, and received life-changing healing.

What happens in your own heart when you hear about a teenager who, because of ministry, stopped cutting herself, or of a couple, teetering on divorce, who receive heart healing and recommit to each other? What price tag do you put on that? How do you measure the joy? How do you measure the cost?

Each of us in RTF ministry have powerful heart-rending stories of God's healing. Sharing these often fans the flame within us to see the least to the greatest be touched by His love.

The question, "Is it really 'worth it?'" has been answered many times through testimonies such as this one which came from a woman who recently found her way to RTF. Following the RTF recommendations, she asked a small group of intercessors to pray for her before, during, and after her ministry. Each day, after her session, she updated them about her experience. Later, she sent her completed 'report' to us as well. Please enjoy her fresh and gripping story.

A Week With An RTF Ministry Team[1]
'Pat'

It is majorly difficult to put into words how intensely the Holy Spirit wove throughout my spirit, soul, and body the redemptive work Jesus personally paid for me out of obedience to His Father. The week that I spent in Hendersonville at Restoring The Foundations ministry surpassed all my expectations: exceeding way beyond any thoughts of wholeness I ever imagined.

Day 1: Penetrating Interview
Day 2: Removing Sins of the Fathers
Day 3: Healing Spirit/Soul Hurts
Day 4: Replacing Ungodly Beliefs with NEW Godly Beliefs
Day 5: Eliminating Demonic Oppression

---

[1] Testimony used by permission.

Day 1

Almost instantly when walking into the ministry room, I knew I was totally safe with my ministry team and the Holy Spirit - with whatever I confessed or whatever may be revealed. The sweet gentleness of the interview was oh so affirming - greatly encouraging my heart.

After the allotted three hours, both ministers asked if I could spend an extra hour with them to tie up some loose ends from my 21 page "My Story" application form (plus several additional pages of personal comments).

I was clueless how revealing to them that application form had been concerning the depths of deception that had become my norm. Their questions to me that afternoon revealed mega evidence of their commitment to pray and seek the wisdom of God for my healing and freedom, before ever meeting me. Surprisingly, it was not my gift of gab that created the need for a longer session - simply lots of issues!

Day 2

Praying through my 21 page My Story, my ministry team had realized my life had been negatively influenced by Freemasonry curses (infirmities/specifically MS). They walked me through each step of renouncing Freemasonry - applying the Blood of Christ to the primary Masonic vows and curses.

Outrageously AMAZING! It was like the weight of a truck being lifted off my shoulders when Satan lost that 'legal' ground. After that HUGE victory, I gained more ground as other strongholds were identified, recognized, confessed, and forgiven.

Throughout the afternoon the three of us were working with the Holy Spirit seeking the "what next?" Once again, my team hung in with me for several hours past the 'allotted' time. Each of us found the Holy Spirit's ministry to heal joyfully invigorating.

Day 3

OUCH! But in a good way. Was it work? 'YES." Was it painful? 'YES.' Was it worth it? 'YES!'

This day was different from the day before in that I was asked to allow the Holy Spirit to specifically reveal to ME what wound was of the most urgency on Father's heart, while they prayed quietly - quietly encouraging me.

Two traumas, which I had no insight how to deal with, lit up like neon signs within my heart; each one was revealed separately, then dealt with separately.

In the 2nd grade: the stronghold of Pat being a BURDEN took root and spread weeds of all kinds in the garden of my young innocent heart. Patiently, the Holy Spirit walked me through healing the trauma; then shattering the stronghold - a sweet victory. I received a vision: a twisted rope hanging from heaven began unraveling - unraveling issue after issue throughout my life until the rope vanished into nothingness.

The last week of 3rd grade: I was brutally molested resulting in bloody panties. I carried all the confusion surrounding this trauma without any available person to share it with. Why? Because of fear of it being my fault in some crazy way. AND because the following day my mother left in an ambulance as I walked to school (I did not see her again until school started the next fall. She spent the entire summer in the hospital).

The stronghold of shame - having been made dirty - planted layers of deceitful seeds in my heart. The seeds perpetuated into false concepts about myself. These beliefs opened the way for me to make many wrong choices. It was beyond my understanding why I had that tendency.

Where was Jesus that afternoon?

He was with me in the thick of it - protecting me - getting me out of the environment before greater pain could happen.

Day 4

This day was WORK with powerful rewards. Little was I aware of how the traumas and failures in my life provided me abundant resources to form belief patterns for survival. Those false beliefs developed into my norm for handling anything life could throw at me; be it through manipulation or evasiveness, or victim mentality.

HALLELUJAH! Being safe to recognize and confess those 14 strongholds; then to walk through forgiving myself (and others) for such blatant deception was work - work done in God's tangible presence.

God's Word powerfully penetrated the darkness, exposing and expelling multiple conglomerations of satanic lies. Now I am consciously replacing each of those incorrect beliefs with Godly Beliefs - passionately searching for "whatever things be of good report."

Many of y'all have repeatedly witnessed through my defensive reactions and comments that I believed it to be impossible for me to ever be good enough to satisfy my husband. **OUCH!** This is now my prayer based on glorious new Truth given to me as I listened to the Holy Spirit's whisper.

> I pray that the perfect love of God which contains no fear or regrets or resentment will penetrate my heart, divinely piercing it in such a way that I can grasp my husband's love for me and for me to realize how deeply I love him.

Day 5

Yep, still about a dozen more remaining strongholds - each with its associated demons - needing death blows. Gratefully, the hardiest roots had been nullified days before by the Blood of Christ. Time was on my side.

My ministers, and I, knew Jesus had spoiled principalities and powers making a show of them, openly triumphing over them in it. I recognized, confessed, and repented from each and every one of them. Jesus discarded them to His place of choosing.

Was Deliverance a walk in the park? Far from it. Demons have one mission: to steal, kill, and destroy. Each demon was not willing to give up its ground without a fight, even when it had legally lost the ground. But Praise THE Lord - spiritually, my "inner hard drive" has been divinely 'rebooted.' I have and am using Godly weapons to torment disarmed demons that want to speak lies to me about my Deliverance.

THROUGHOUT the week I had experienced the lessening of the MS symptoms - I had immediate relief after breaking the Masonic curse. Also, another RTF team who had a specific heart for physical healing set aside time to pray with me before my last afternoon session. It was an incredibly precious time of prayer and discernment - such wisdom flowed through each of them to me.

Absolutely awesome! As we prayed, I was blessed with a vision of the darkest-darkness being scattered by the most-'mostest' brilliant LIGHT. At that very moment I actually felt my diaphragm engaging with my lungs to empty out the carbon dioxide so my lungs could fill with oxygen and effectively distribute it - meaning the damaged nerves from MS lesions in my brain were healed.

Jesus HEALED me!

REJOICE, AND AGAIN, I SAY REJOICE! After 20 years of progressive MS disabilities, I am no longer using my forearm crutches to walk outside the house to wherever. I am relearning to lift my knee, raise my foot/toes, and step forward. I am strengthening the leg and ankle muscles. AND my neurologist has given me permission to stop using my Bipap which I had to use eight hours/night in order to get up and function the following morning.

My body needs rebuilding. The nerves in my brain need to remember their job descriptions. This is happening. The symptoms continue to diminish. God designed us to be healthy inside-out; recipients of Divine love and healing. I am committed to continue to do what is necessary to fully receive my healing.

Freedom

Chapter 25
Our Inner Journey

Clearly for us our outer journey to establish a Training Center was largely fueled by our own inward journey. The horrendous outpouring of energy it took to locate Echo Mountain Inn, the sharing of the vision and the raising of funds, the developing of a curriculum, even putting up with the lousy loan shark, all came from a deep passion birthed by God first healing and transforming our lives. Ever since He had so deeply touched us, we lived with a burning desire to provide a place where that could happen for others as well. Now it was happening.

Even the wonderful words 'healing' and 'freedom' do not quite encompass or describe the potential depth of change that can occur. It's more than just having a few burdens lifted and a fresh measure of peace, as profound and welcome as these things are. Our passion had to do with a "God change," a qualitative change in how our hearts and our spirits respond to Him. When a "God change" occurs, a place of fresh intimacy with Father, Son and Holy Spirit develops, a place of powerful connectedness. One's entire life focus shifts into living a life together with God; in His Presence, in His mystery, in a flow of communication and communion. One simply wants to go about life abiding in Him.

A "God change" had happened to us. God came into our own places of abandonment and regret. He came into those festering areas where we thought we were not good enough, that we would never measure up. He blasted through our shame and began to remove it. He came into our anger, our lust, our fearfulness, and trauma. As He moved what we thought were immovable mountains out of our lives, our hearts changed. Never again would we be the same.

"God change" causes us to realign ourselves with the very person we were created to be. The experience of salvation is fleshed out. Now our hearts beat in rhythm with His heart. Now we live in partnership with Him, as Firstborn Sons.

Let's have a place where we can learn to set the table for others to encounter Him. We saw that using the RTF Integrated Approach to Healing helps set that table, because it is designed for each person to hear God in every individual session. It contains the potential of encounter. Our prayer was (and is), "Lord, let this Inn and Training Center be places where people meet with You, are transformed, and live in Your Presence."

Can you imagine our excitement as Bishop Bill Hamon spoke these words to us and the Inn at the time of the Inn's dedication? "The Lord declares, 'This place is My Footstool. My Presence is here and will abide here. All who come are invited to partake of My Presence and to abide in My Presence. My Presence will always rest here with you.'"

The Lord knew our hearts. He was describing exactly what we yearned for the most.

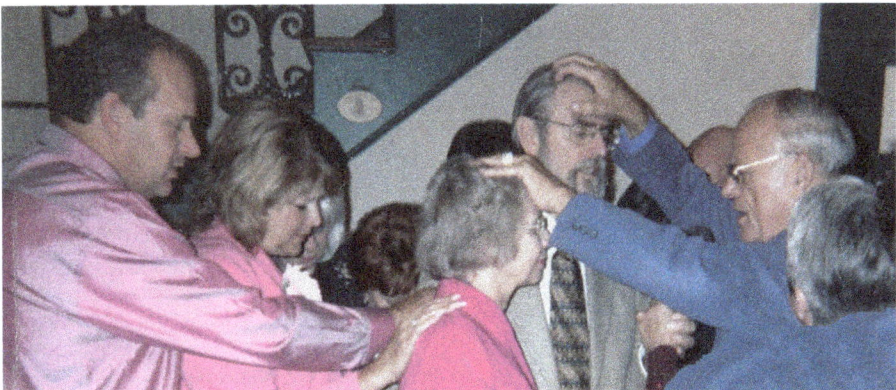

Bishop Bill Hamon praying for the Kylstras at the dedication of the RTF International Training Center at Echo Mountain Inn in October, 2005.

Our wonderful 70th Birthday Celebrations.
Family: Pam Kylstra, James Davis, and Lewis Davis.
Friends: Dorathy Railey and Polly Altman.

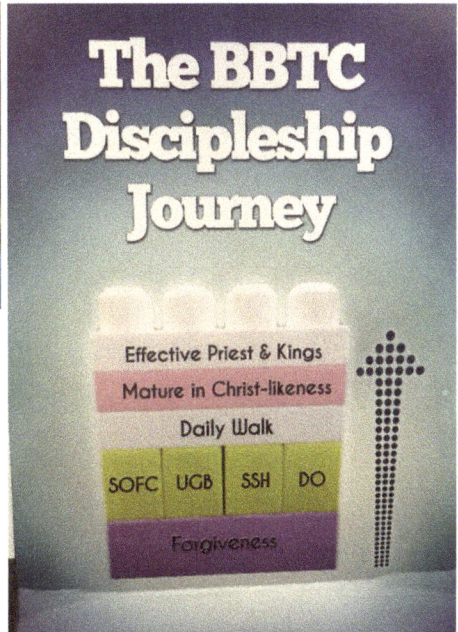

The BBTC Discipleship Journey

Effective Priest & Kings
Mature in Christ-likeness
Daily Walk
SOFC | UGB | SSH | DO
Forgiveness

Following Pastor David Lee, Judah and Hephizbah Choo assumed the leadership of RTF Asia Pacific. In a few short years God has used them to greatly multiple the number of Issue-Focused Ministers.

SPECIAL MOMENTS – SPECIAL PEOPLE

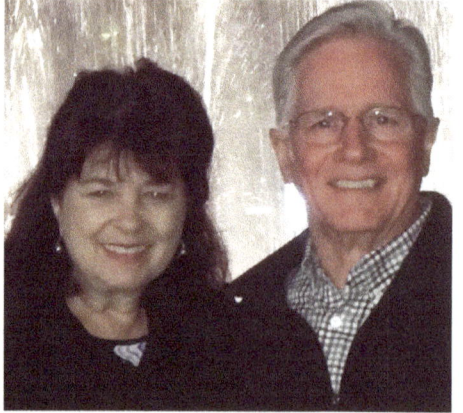

Faces seen around the Inn: Paul Fitzgerald, Kim Butler; Pauline Ezell, Tom and Paulette Garman; Tim and Anne Evans, and Mike and Debbie Sayovitz.

116

PART III
THE INN: TRANSITION

Chapter 26
Just Wait

This part of our story began four or five years before we discovered Echo Mountain Inn, or, "our leap off the high dive," so to speak, to establish our Training Center. This part began in our hearts.

"Lord," we had asked, "do you want this RTF ministry to continue after our lifetime?" Time and again, we heard, "Yes, it is to continue." At first we were almost afraid to trust what we were hearing. Periodically, we would ask again. His answer was always a resounding, "Yes, it is to continue." And so we kept moving, planning for sustainability.

"And who are our successors?" came our next direct question to the Lord. For years we heard the same answer. "You don't know them yet. Just wait." This was not the answer we wanted. Chester is a 'Doer' and I am a 'Planner.' These kind of people do not like "Just wait!" kind of answers. However, God's plans are purposeful and will not be rushed. His timing is seldom our timing. Have you noticed?

"Chester, do you think that couple might be our successor couple?" I would ask, on different occasions. Once again, we would pray and get the unwanted, "Just wait!" answer one more time. Doing all we could to be patient, we continued to lead the ministry. We were very fulfilled as we watched God grow it.

In 2011, seven years after the start of the Training Center, we both heard the Lord's voice regarding our Successors. Here is Chester's account.

> One morning during worship, a few days into a new Training Module II, the Lord spoke to my heart. "See that couple over there?" I opened one eye and looked where He was directing. "Yes, Lord, I see them."

> "They are your Successors." Shocked, my other eye flew open as I stared at these suddenly very important people.

> "Oh yes. Lee and Cindi Whitman." They had come the previous year to Module I training. A nice couple. Seemed to be serious about their Christian walk and relationship with God. "Lord, I think I need to get to know this couple."

In the same time period, the Lord also spoke to me. Cindi was at the podium teaching on Abraham sacrificing Isaac. Her anointed message was deeply touching hearts, including mine. "She can do what you do," the Lord said gently to my heart. "Together, she and Lee can take RTF on to the next generation."

Not saying a word to anyone else, we continued to pray. We begin to place the Whitmans in leadership positions to help them learn about the RTF ministry from the "inside out," and to see how they did at handling different situations. They did well! In many ways, for us, it had become a "done deal" the day the Lord spoke to our hearts. At last our "Just wait!" was over.

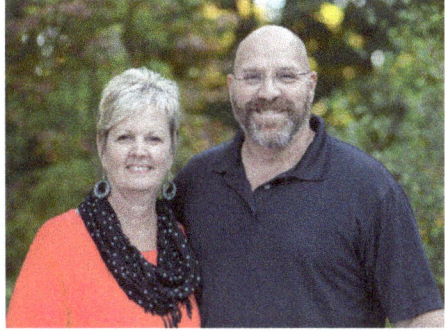

Chapter 27
Our Successors

It was settled. We knew the Lord had chosen Lee and Cindi Whitman. We were both excited and at peace with His choice. In our hearts, we chose them as well. What an amazing couple. They were multi-talented, skilled, and gifted. They could preach and teach, lead and organize. But what we were most drawn to was their decision-making process. It went something like this, "Lord, what are You saying?"

In January 2014, looking for ways to help the people in the Healing House Network begin to know the Whitmans, we asked them to share a message at the RTF International Advanced Conference the coming Fall. "What do you want us to share on?" they inquired immediately. Having yet to decide on the main conference theme, we simply answered, "Oh, just ask the Lord, and see what He says."

For several weeks we had no communication with them. Meanwhile, we were looking for the right opportunity to talk to them face-to-face, to 'pop' the question. Together with the two couples on our Board of Directors, we had been praying about this time and this decision for many months. We all knew this was the time. We planned to meet with them, share the story of our waiting for our Successors, and how God had pointed them out to us; how for several years we had been positioning them to both evaluate them and prepare them for the leadership of RTF. The question we wanted to ask was; "Will you assume the responsibility and privilege of being the Executive Directors of the Restoring The Foundations International Ministries?"

Before we had set a date to meet, however, the Whitmans texted with the title for their message at the fall conference. They wrote, "We believe the title is 'Just say "Yes".'" After that text, Chester and I laughed hilariously. "Do you think maybe, just maybe, God has gone ahead of us and positioned them to "Just say 'Yes'?"

Soon thereafter we agreed to meet in Nashville on a Sunday, early in February, for our "ever so important" question. As usual, we enjoyed the beautiful drive through the Blue Ridge Mountains. We asked the Whitmans to please not tell anyone we were coming, since we only had a little time, not enough to also visit a number of our friends in the Nashville area. We knew the time we did have needed to be private and very focused.

So what was happening in their lives during this same period of time? Here is their story.

Just Say "Yes"
Lee and Cindi Whitman

We were introduced to Restoring the Foundations by our friend James Goll. Our counseling ministry was located in an office that we rented from James. James was holding a conference at his office called "Warfare of the Heart" and he had invited three different healing ministries to make a presentation. Chester and Betsy Kylstra were one of the couples taking part in this conference. I (Lee) had been in Christian counseling for 18 years and had attended many conferences on inner healing over those years and, frankly, didn't see the need to go to one more. However, out of respect to James, we attended. When we heard Chester and Betsy present the four problem/ministry areas and how RTF ministers to them in an integrated way, the Holy Spirit shouted in my ear, "THIS WILL WORK!"

That next January, 2010, we attended Training Module I in Hendersonville. We went back home and did as many Issue-Focused Ministry sessions as we could. We asked anyone who was willing to let us practice taking them through this new ministry we were involved in, and many of them received incredible healing.

The next year, 2011, we came back to the ITC to attend Training Module II. God had different plans and asked us if we would stay and complete Module III as well.

It was during this season that God spoke to us clearly through Genesis 22, the story of Abraham and Isaac. God spoke to us, just as He did to Abraham, that He would provide. Of course, our immediate need was for financial provision. We had no idea that we would also face one of the most challenging family crisis of our lives while we were at the International Training Center. We came to know God as financial provider in a deeper way but we also came to know Father God as provider for our emotional needs, and as provider and protector of our children and our grandchildren. His promise in Gen 22:18 is one that we continued to press into and hold on to: *"All the nations of the earth will be blessed through your offspring, because you have listened to my voice."* It was clear that if we chose to stay in obedience and complete our training, He would use our children and grandchildren to bless the nations. He confirmed in our hearts that our obedience had generational impact. We were tested again and again. Would we trust Him with our children and grandchildren? We said "Yes" to God and stayed for four months of training. All of our bills were miraculously paid by the end. By His strength and faithfulness to meet us along the way we learned to trust Him in greater measure.

After completing Training Modules II and III, and being accepted into the Healing House Network, we returned home to Nashville, Tennessee. We began doing RTF ministry full-time.

Over the next few years we realized that we were being given an unusual amount of favor by the RTF leadership. Frankly, in the natural, we knew we didn't deserve the favor we were experiencing. We had only been a part of RTF for a short time. Part of that favor was being given the opportunity to go to Kona, Hawaii, two years in a row to be part of the training at YWAM. We also were asked to take the lead of a Training Module I at the International Training Center. We loved RTF and were glad for any opportunity to be involved in training more ministers.

Then in February of 2014, we received a phone call from Chester and Betsy asking if they could come visit us in Nashville. They had a question they wanted to ask us, but they didn't want anyone else to know they were coming. Our immediate thought was, "What have we done that is so bad that Chester and Betsy have to come all the way to Nashville to correct us?" We prayed about it and could not think of anything we had done that was 'that' wrong. And even if we had done something wrong, they would have to forgive us because forgiveness is part of RTF ministry; "Right?"

We had about ten days between when the Kylstras called and their actual visit. So, we began to pray. We wanted to have our hearts right for whatever it was that they would ask. During that same time period Betsy texted asking for the title of our message that we had been invited to present at the Advanced Conference that year. So, we prayed about that as well. God gave us a title that we texted back to Betsy.

The morning they were going to arrive we still did not have peace about their visit and what we were to say to them; so we spent the morning out on the back porch praying. We had no idea what they were going to ask us. If we are being very honest, we went to the worst case scenario. It had to do with Mozambique. We had had several Iris missionaries training at the ITC that year, so we wondered if they might ask us to go to Mozambique for 2-3 years and establish a RTF training school there. Now Iris is a wonderful ministry and we love being involved with them, and Mozambique is certainly a needful mission field. However, Cindi really likes hot and cold running water, she likes her blow-dryer and Lee really likes air conditioning. He likes it a lot! Mozambique just does not align with these comforts of civilization.

So that morning, out on the back porch, our prayer was, "Lord, please adjust our hearts so that they are right for whatever the Kylstras ask us to do. How do you want us to answer them, Lord?" God clearly spoke to Cindi and said, "Do you remember the title to that message you are presenting at the Advanced Conference? That is what I want you to answer!" The title of the message was, "Just Say Yes!" We struggled with the idea of moving away from our family and friends and possibly to a place without all the comforts of home, but we had reached a place of total surrender to do whatever God asked of us through Chester and Betsy.

What an amazing Father God we have. He also told us that morning, "You are not going to feel qualified to do what they ask you. You are going to ask, 'Why us?' But whatever they ask you I want you to 'Just Say Yes!'" We knew our answer before we even knew the question. And the question they asked us was not a question we ever would have imagined.

You see, we had never considered that they would ask us to be their successors. If there had been an application process for the position, we would not have applied. We would have disqualified ourselves from that position. After all, we have not been doing RTF as long as a lot of other people. We did not think we had what it took to succeed people like the Kylstras and run an international ministry. Plus, we were very happy and seeing some wonderful fruit doing RTF ministry in Nashville. We think that is why God gave us the answer to the question before we even knew the question. God knew that we didn't see ourselves as He sees us.

When they arrived and asked us if we would consider being their successors and lead RTF, we were shocked to say the least. After we talked about what being their successor would "look like" for a while, they asked if we would like to take some time to think and pray before giving them our answer. Instead of taking days to consider our answer, we went for a walk around the neighborhood and prayed. During that walk God reminded us about the conversation on the porch that morning. He reminded us that He said to "**Just Say Yes"** to whatever they asked. So, we returned from our walk and said "Yes!" And we continue to choose to say "Yes" to God every day.

TRANSITION

Chapter 28
Transition

How we would have liked to have had a Big Book of detailed guidelines about the best way to manage a major transition in leadership. Oh yes, that would have been so helpful. This non-existent book is needed both for the current leaders as well as for the new leaders preparing to assume their position. Mostly, what we had heard about, or observed ourselves, were heartbreaking failures. We actually felt clearer about how to prepare the network and make a place for the Whitmans than how to make this big physical and emotional change for ourselves. The One Thing we could count on was this: the same Lord who had given us the RTF revelation initially, the same Lord who for years had opened doors for us supernaturally, the same Lord who had directed us to the Inn and fulfilled the vision He had given to us, was still in charge. He was still directing our path and would carry us both through the transition and the coming years ahead. We had always felt like stewards, not owners, of what He had given. Having peace on most days, we moved forward.

Chester and I agreed that we wanted to personally call and share this news with many of the dear friends who had been with us in ministry for years. Even though we did not have enough time to call everyone, we wanted to call as many people in the Healing House Network as we could, as well as call the leaders of the networks we had served. As we approached the end of the second week of what felt like nonstop communication, we knew we were doing the right thing.

Hearing this big news, some said, "We are so proud of what you have done, and that you are honoring us by sharing this with us personally." Several others burst into tears, expressing their heartfelt connection to us, and sharing their fears about what was to come. Still others, knowing that we were already well past

127

the age for normal retirement, expressed much gratitude that we weren't leaving them or the network in a time of crisis, but were putting a good plan into place for everyone's protection. Almost all said, "We have always trusted that you hear the Lord and we trust you now." It was an exhausting, exhilarating heart-rending two weeks. The transition was in motion.

Knowing how important face-to-face contact is, we provided an opportunity for Lee and Cindi to travel with us to each RTF region and to share their story. We wanted people to see their faces, to hear their hearts, and to begin to know them BEFORE we passed the baton. We each told our part of the story. Lee and Cindi were very well received. Looking back, we now know that these contacts were a very important part of the preparation for transition.

Chapter 29
Passing The Baton

The atmosphere was electric, charged with the Lord's Presence. Lumps were in our throats as the processional began. David and Amy Boersmas, dear friends and gifted worship leaders, were positioned on the stage. From our front row seats, we turned and watched a sea of colorful flags, more than twenty flags, waving, moving forward, in a stately but thrilling procession. The carriers

of those flags deserved to be proud, for most of them were RTF HHN members representing their own nations. Their hearts had joined with ours in wanting to see the people of their nation set free. These flags spoke of our history with each individual carrying them. These flags spoke of having an RTF spiritual stake in the ground of their nation. "Twenty, Lord, twenty!" I exclaimed. These flags represented God's goodness as He had sustained us and brought so many wonderful people to walk by our sides. Overwhelmed with gratitude, I finished the worship song, probably far away from the real tune, but my heart was very much in tune.

We shared our messages, the evening progressed, and now it was time for the Passing of the Baton, a moment we had anticipated for so many months. We knew that this moment was significant both in the heavenlies and on the earth, because, about two months earlier, Chester had said to me one morning:

> You know, as we get ready for this "Passing of the Baton" ceremony, as we call it, we need to make it a significant event in the natural as well as in the supernatural. You see, I was awakened suddenly in the middle of the night last night. As I came awake, I suddenly 'knew' that the Lord wanted us to use a special baton as we performed the ceremony. He wanted us to use a 'real' baton, not some plastic rod used in a relay race, or twirled by a majorette. As I lay there, absorbing what I had just experienced, I realized that I did not know what a 'real' baton was. So I got up and did an internet search. I won't take the time to tell you what I learned, but it is clear that batons have played a significant role throughout history in the passing of authority and power. The special ones are of wood, several feet long, and beautifully finished.

> I searched the internet for a suitable baton. Most are very expensive, but I found a really neat one on eBay at a good price. It is two and a half feet long, an inch in diameter, wood, and well finished. We should have it in a few days. We can use gold paint to put the name of the ministry on it, as well as our names and the Whitman's names. There will be plenty of room to add more leaders in the future. We are going to use a 'real' baton!

As the time came, a holy hush fell over our friends in the audience. Lee and Cindi stood silently before us. For just a moment, we paused as together, all four of us held the baton.

It was a significant moment. The baton was more than a 'baton.' It represented all of our dreams and pioneering. It represented years of caring for our people in the HHN network and beyond. It held our hopes for the ministry's future. It meant Lee and Cindi were answering God's call to lead. We released our hands. The shift was made. Now the baton was out of our hands and into theirs. I exhaled deeply. It was done.

From now on we would function primarily as the head of the Board of Directors. Our role as day-by-day leaders was complete.

"Lord, take them on. Watch over them as You have watched over us. Give them divine open doors, divine appointments and divine favor. Help them fulfill all that You desire for them and for this ministry to become."

Group by group, those who had been previously invited came to the stage to surround Lee and Cindi, to pray and bless them, and to commit to support them. With each new group, I felt a fresh wave of emotion. Our Board of Directors, our local and area pastors, our Regional Directors, our International Leaders, our staff, and lastly, a group of young generation leaders, came to bless them. This last group included Matilda, Jessica, Khanh, Ashley, Peter, and others. We had contended for this younger generation. They had been touched. Now, they have become young leaders with us. At this very moment they were standing with Lee and Cindi. Many of the people hugged us, or touched our hands, as they passed by.

As this moving event was happening, a hymn that had been part of my life from my growing up years welled up in my memory:

> God of the marching centuries,
> Lord of the marching years,
> Leading a people's victories,
> Sharing a people's tears,
> Seal us as now we worship
> Thee, here on this moment's height;
> Star of the way our fathers found,
> Be still our guiding Light.

"Yes, Lord. This is a very high moment. And Yes, You are still our guiding Light."

The evening ended with what for us was a total surprise, a very honoring surprise. The Whitmans, the RTF Board, and leadership teams presented us with a wonderful book including letters of appreciation and testimonies from people around the world. This has become a treasure we often keep on our coffee table. In addition, a beautiful crystal figure of hands holding up the world was given to us. Its meaningful inscription read, "You made a World of Difference Restoring the Body of Christ." It is placed in our dining room where we can frequently enjoy it. Lastly, the most unexpected of all, was a monetary gift, a large gift from many friends from around the world. We were astounded, too overwhelmed to say more than a simple "Thank you." The audience, our friends, exploded in a standing ovation.

Driving home that night, we were quiet. It was hard to take in the magnitude of what had just happened. We knew it would take time. However, one thing we agreed on there and then: We would use the financial love gift from our friends on something very special (and we have).

PART IV
AFTER THE INN

Chapter 30
Change

For many years, Chester and I have lived out of John 10:10, where Jesus says, "I have come that you might have life, and have it more abundantly." My personal translation of "abundantly" is to live life fully charged and over the top. That looks different in each season of our lives. Currently a treasured dimension is discretionary time. We delight in spending it with children, grandchildren, and friends. With the love gift given to us at the baton passing, we have been thrilled to buy a small travel trailer and an upgraded car to pull it. Travel and camping provide a wonderful new freedom.

As Chairman of the Board of Directors, we stay involved with Restoring The Foundations ministry in a significant way. The board, legally responsible for the ministry, provides a place of undergirding for the Directors as well as being a place for them to incubate new ideas and have the guidance of checks and balances. And so we move forward together.

The RTF vision hasn't changed, but the form and format in which it is delivered is in the process of change. RTF must be delivered in a way that is relevant for each new generation. Relevant equals alive, engaging, workable, and affordable. This principle holds true in every organization, whether business or ministry.

For many people, 'Change' is a "four letter word." Research tells us that only a very small minority of people actually celebrate change. The great majority of us face it, but sometimes with tears. Another small minority resists change all together, and often gets left behind. For most of us, change is not easy.

Everyone who is a part of RTF is being impacted by change. Have you noticed? In addition to having new Directors at the helm, we have also reached a place in our new season where we believe God would have us release our Grand Old Lady, Echo Mountain Inn. For those who have received RTF training here, or even personal, life changing ministry, this is particularly difficult. It is requiring a lot of courage.

Why does this change need to happen? First, the Board, including the Whitmans, believe that RTF will be able to expand our army more effectively if our base is decentralized, with training modules being offered in many locations. Secondly, our Inn has always needed financial supplementation. In the past two years, the extra funds for "making up the difference" have not "been there." In their well-written email[1] to the network in the spring of 2017, the Whitmans drew a parallel between where the ministry is now and Elijah at the brook Cherith. When the brook dried up, Elijah knew that it was time to move on. Our supplementary funds had simply dried up. In the distance, we can hear the shofar sounding. It is time to pull up our tent pegs and move out. It takes courage to move out. With the Lord's empowerment, we have the courage to do so.

We would like Lee and Cindi to share their story about selling Echo Mountain Inn and their thoughts about the future.

Into the Future
Lee and Cindi Whitman

Selling Echo Mountain Inn

The decision to sell Echo Mountain Inn was not an easy one. We have a lot of wonderful memories of our own healing and freedom that took place at EMI. We have memories with friends and memories of challenges that are connected to EMI. We know that our memories do not even begin to compare with the

---

[1] A copy of this email is in Appendix B on page 146.

memories of dozens of others who have invested much in time and financial resources into Echo Mountain Inn.

The journey to the decision began when we had an architect come do a feasibility study on the property owned by RTF, which includes Echo Mountain Inn and some adjacent land. We wanted to know what would be involved in building a facility that would accommodate proper Training Rooms, Ministry Rooms and offices for RTF. We had outgrown Classroom One! The report of the architect was not encouraging. Due to a number of factors, he recommended that we sell and start over. He said he couldn't recommend building on that site due to the staggering costs that would be involved, even though it meant that he would be losing our business in designing the building we wanted.

We tucked away that report and prayed, "Lord what do we do? RTF is set for massive explosion but our current facilities are 'locked in.' We can't grow and expand without a larger facility for training."

In January of 2017, at a gathering with several of our leaders, they brought up the topic of selling the Inn. We hadn't mentioned it at all. As we dialoged they shared their concerns and observations. We decided that it wouldn't be prudent to talk about 'where' to move the ministry, but over the next several hours we developed criteria that we agreed were characteristics needed in a new location for RTF.

Over the next couple of months our eyes were opened to other things that underscored our need to sell Echo Mountain Inn and to move the headquarters of RTF to another location. On one particularly difficult day, Cindi was struggling with the situation. "Lord, why are we being asked to present the idea of selling the Inn to Chester and Betsy and the Board of Directors?" We knew how much their hearts and vision for RTF were connected to the Inn. We knew it would not be an easy thing to ask. Cindi cried out to the Lord, "Why would You ask us to do this? We've only just begun as the leaders of RTF." With tears streaming down her face, Cindi heard Father's voice whisper, "Because I knew you'd do it and it's time."

With His confirming words, we began the dialog with the Board and Chester and Betsy. On March 20, 2017, the RTF Board of Directors unanimously voted to sell Echo Mountain Inn. It was the first day of spring, a day of new beginnings.

What's Next?
As we traveled over the next months there were questions. Of course, everyone wanted to know where the new RTF Headquarters would be. We asked them to share their thoughts. We expressed that we were keeping a list of impressions and prophetic words, looking for Father God to confirm the new location. We chose not to share the location that was burning in our hearts. We wanted the location to be confirmed by the voice of many and not just from our own heart's desire.

Within five months we received suggestions for three different locations for RTF headquarters. One location was mentioned 12 different times through texts, zoom calls, conversations and prophetic words. (Eleven times more than the other two.) The city mentioned met all of the criteria developed by our leadership group. The location is a city with world-wide attention through sports, media, and music. It is a city that is open to inner healing. It is a city that is alive spiritually. It is a city where RTF has already made an impact and has a growing number of IFM and TF ministers. It is a city within five hours of eight other large cities (Cincinnati, St. Louis, Indianapolis, Lexington, Louisville, Memphis, Birmingham and Atlanta).

Prophetic Words

One of the words received was from Sue Mead. "The Lord told me about five years ago that He has given Nashville to RTF. I told Betsy and she heartily agreed." Linda Roeder shared that she was praying about other things related to RTF when she heard "Nashville." She said she wasn't even asking about a location. Dave confirmed as he prayed that Nashville seemed like a good possibility. Another prophetic word from a personal intercessor was, "The light is shining on Nashville. The Lord is going to use RTF to bring restoration to the hearts and lives of many in the limelight. Restoration will transform the city and it will be broadcast throughout the world through the songs penned from those whose hearts are healed."

The Lord sent us to Nashville in 1988. It was His plan for us to raise our family, to minister, to grow and learn in that city. In the process we developed 29 years of relationships in the Christian community. This will obviously now benefit RTF. We felt we had the confirmation we needed to move back to Nashville. The RTF Board confirmed this decision in August 2017.

So, as of the time of this writing, the decision has been made to establish the new RTF headquarters and future International Training Center in or around metro Nashville, TN. Obviously, there are many questions about the future and what it will look like. However, we do know that we all have a mandate from Father God to take RTF to the nations. We know that in this next season there be multiple locations for RTF Training Centers throughout the world. Father God has not yet fully revealed the specifics of His next phase blueprint for RTF but we are responding one step at a time by "**Just Saying YES**."

(Continue Kylstras...) Visible change is happening! After having been an important part of RTF, the Fortiers have moved back to Vermont. Ed and Dawn Shields, following the Fortiers, have come in with lots of energy and new ideas. There are new faces in the RTF office as well; Jaque Orsi and Melanie Johnson are there every day (along with Susan).

New leaders are taking their places as Area Directors, and HHN members continue to define and re-define the roles they feel called to play.

A strong community remains here in Hendersonville and nearby areas. Some of us have friendships of ten or more years. Steve and Lorie Hart will bring fresh unity and connectedness as they lead in the years ahead.

The day will come when we have to say a tender good-by to our Inn. We have cherished her, and all that she gave us. We know, however, that the RTF ministry is not a building, not a location, but it is us – the entire group of us. It is a living relationship between us and the Lord – as we serve to bring His healing. With all the change, that hasn't changed.

The future looks more than promising. However, before we move on and out, we would like to take a moment to pause and celebrate you. Most of you reading this book have sown substantially into the RTF ministry for years. Your seeds have produced bushels and baskets of fruit. Abundant fruit. Now your generous seeds are ready to multiply once again, to spring up in new places. Your seeds, that have already helped raise an army of capable ministers, are further expanding and extending to the world. Nothing has been wasted! We are expectant.

We look to the future with much excitement, continuing to say "Yes, Lord." Our passion for the Lord and for His healing is stronger than ever. Many members of our generation look to retirement years, not as "do-nothing" years, but as a special time to share the riches of our lives already well lived. Now approaching or in the eighties, the Sherrerds, Brisbins, Briggs, Valleys, ourselves and others are ministering as opportunities arise. Lewis Smith, 89, ministers frequently and powerfully. Why not?

We believe that all of us who are called as RTF ministers are also called to live out of John 10:10. Together, as part of God's healing army, we will move ahead, with different battalions, in different locations. We will all be listening to the Master's voice, living our lives to the fullest, "over the top.

APPENDICES

APPENDIX A
HISTORY OF ECHO MOUNTAIN INN

The Inn was built by John H. and Jessie B. Patterson of Jacksonville, Florida, as a private summer home in 1896. It was purchased in the 1920s by Felix Lake and then Dr. Charles and Ida deGarmo, also from Florida. They operated it as "The Tea Room" until Florida hurricanes and the 1929 stock market crash caused them to close the doors. Then Florida friends convinced Isabel J. Foster to lease the property. With considerable ingenuity and hard work, she and her daughter, Nell, operated "Camp Happiness" for teenage girls for four seasons. She bought cots for $0.25 each and turned the porches and all available space into dormitories. Isabel also created a swimming pool from an abandoned reservoir, set up tennis courts and hiking trails, and provided horseback riding lessons.

In the mid 1930s, the Royall family bought the property from the deGarmos. Rev. William R. Royall, his wife, Ina, and his son, William Jr., named it Echo Inn and ran it as a restaurant and country Inn until the 1970s. They made additions to the main Inn and built several other buildings on the property. William R. Royall Jr. also served as mayor of Laurel Park Village for 17 years.

For the next 20 years, the Inn, which became known as Echo Mountain Inn, had several owners including Cooper and Elizabeth Smith, Dick and Marion Mulford, and Peter and Shirley Demaras. Each made additions and improvements based on their talents and vision for the Inn.

In July 2004, the Inn was purchased by Restoring The Foundations International ministries. This ministry has both operated it as a Bed and Breakfast Inn open to the public and as the ministry Headquarters. It has been a perfect place for many to come for personal ministry and training.

The ministry has worked very hard to keep the historic character of the property while adding modern conveniences. Each newly restored and decorated room has been named to convey its unique motif. From the Royal Room to the Plum Pretty Room to the Rustic Room, every effort has been made to provide a place where the guest will feel at home.

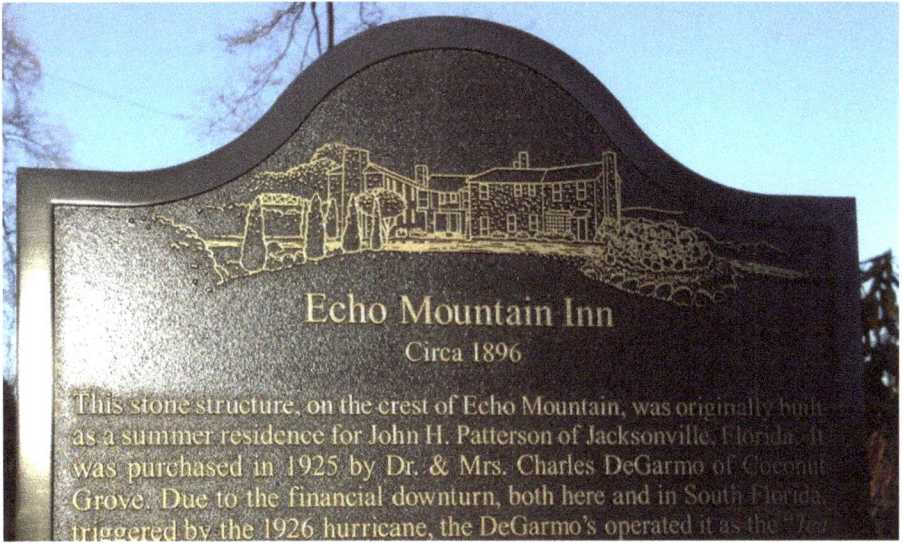

Plaque commemorating Echo Mountain
Inn's history; located near Entrance Gate.

RESTORING THE FOUNDATIONS
———— INTERNATIONAL ————

2849 Laurel Park Highway - Hendersonville, NC, 28739
Office@RestoringTheFoundations.org   www.RestoringTheFoundations.org
828-696-9075

APPENDIX B
EMAIL TO HEALING HOUSE NETWORK MEMBERS

March 22, 2017

Dear Ones,

At the International Advanced Conference in Sept. 2015 we were given the responsibility of stewarding Restoring the Foundations International Ministry and Echo Mountain Inn. We take the responsibility of being good stewards of the Ministry and all that has been put in our hands very seriously. Our goal and mandate from the Lord is to lead RTF forward and to expand the Ministry and Training of RTF worldwide. RTF is on the edge of breakthrough and explosive expansion but some things are holding us back.

As we have sought the Lord he has continuously reminded us of the story of Elijah at the brook Cherith. God provided miraculously for Elijah during that season but then the season changed. Elijah's provision dried up. He was forced to leave the place of provision that God had originally given to him. As he listened God spoke and Elijah was given the next instructions to obey. God continued to provide through an unlikely source, the widow of Nain. She had very little to give but she responded out of a heart of love and she sacrificially gave her last meal of provision to Elijah. In the midst of his obedience to move away from Cherith, both Elijah and the widow received the blessing and provision from God. Their miracles were connected!

We believe that it is time for us to take a step of obedience along with all of you to release the miracle outpouring of abundant blessings to RTF and to the network.

Echo Mountain Inn has served as a wonderful place for RTF Ministry and Training to be birthed and to grow. Many people have had a significant encounter with Father God and have experienced healing of their hearts at Echo Mountain Inn. It has been a place to come and receive training and it helped establish RTF as a respected ministry worldwide and provided a place to bask in the healing presence. Many of **you** have given sacrificially of your time and your finances to Echo Mountain Inn as a blessing to RTF. Most of us have wonderful memories of our time at Echo Mountain Inn. It has been beneficial for a season but we believe that season has passed.

It was always in the plans of Chester and Betsy to expand the Training facilities, to build a meeting area, Ministry offices and meeting rooms on the property that is owned by RTF. We had an architect do a feasibility study on the possibility of expanding. It has been determined that it is not an option to build as originally planned. So, it is with sadness and yet great expectation that we want to inform you that the decision has been made to sell Echo Mountain Inn. This was not a decision that came easily for any of us. We all have fond memories of past events, of the early beginnings, or of our days in training together. This was a unanimous decision by the RTF Board: Chester and Betsy Kylstra, Ray and Emily Duenke, Dave and Linda Roeder and Lee and Cindi Whitman.

Our hope and prayer focus is that you will join us by praying in a buyer quickly so that we are able to reap the full benefits of the investment of time, money, and resources that have been poured into Echo Mountain Inn by so many. A quick sale will allow us have the finances for the next steps. It is our hope and prayer that you will continue to financially support RTF during this season of ongoing transition.

Echo Mountain Inn has been the home of RTFI and the International Training Center but it is not RTF.

RTF Ministry will continue to grow, flourish and thrive in this next season. Our goal and vision is to expand our Training facilities to continue to offer excellent training for RTF ministers and to provide a place for ongoing healing for many, and do it in a debt free facility.

There are a lot of questions about the future that we do not have answers for at this time. We are taking small steps and asking God for the revelation about where to move RTFI Headquarters.

Concerning the staff of Echo Mountain Inn:
Greg and Stephanie Fortier have felt for some time that there was a new season coming for them. They have been tremendously faithful during these last 13 years as they have given and served sacrificially. They initiated a conversation with us in November of 2015 and told us that they didn't want us to feel guilty or carry false responsibility if the Lord told us to move RTFI headquarters to another location. Interestingly, today (Monday) Greg and Steph told us that they have an opportunity to move on. They will be finishing up their commitment to EMI and RTF at the end of the Training this year. It seems that the Lord is preparing things ahead of us.

We would like to be able to bless Greg and Stephanie as well as the other employees of EMI. We have asked the EMI staff to stay until we sell or until we make the decision to close the doors. It is our hearts desire to be able to bless each of them financially for their time of sacrifice and dedication to EMI and to RTF. (Tim Turner, Jessica Hutcher, Ashlyn McGinnis, Gabe and Marly Urzo, and Sally Boneau) *Would you begin praying that Father God would provide their next employment at just the right time?*

Concerning the staff of RTF:
We do not anticipate any staff changes at this time. As the Lord reveals the future plans for RTF we will all know more. Our staff is small. Mark Buckman, and Lee and I are the only fulltime employees of RTF. The remainder of the staff: Jaque and Marcelo Orsi, Susan Rhodes, Melanie Johnson, Bob and Cheria Guier and Stephanie Fortier are all part-time staff. As the Lord reveals the future home for RTFI Headquarters we will know more. The amazing thing is many of the things that we all do can be done from anywhere in the world via technology. Of course we want a place to call home for RTFI and we believe that God will lead us there in the right time.

This is difficult for all of us. We did not come to this decision lightly. We are sad and yet we have great expectation that the best is yet ahead.

We have the opportunity to dream with God for the future of RTF!

Will you join us in expectation for God's Miracle provision? Will you ask God to send a buyer quickly? Will you ask Him to provide new employment opportunities for the EMI staff?

We are expectant and hopeful for the future that He has for us! The best days are yet ahead!

Many blessings,

Lee and Cindi Whitman

Supported by and in agreement with:
Chester and Betsy Kylstra
Dave and Linda Roeder
Ray and Emily Duenke

Author's Biography

When Chester and Betsy heard God's call on their lives, the biblical passage about, "two becoming one" took on new meaning. Already well established in their careers of Aerospace Engineering and Mental Health Counseling, they left that behind and began to work together as teachers and ministers in the Body of Christ.

During their first year in Bible College, God did a deep healing and deliverance work in them both culminating in the revelation of the "Integrated Approach to Healing". They immediately began sharing what they were learning with others and training other couples to bring the healing and freedom to church members.

Since 1990, when they began to minister full-time, God has continued to expand their vision. Many others have joined with them to fulfill the vision of bringing forth a Bride without spot or wrinkle.

Later, in 1994, the Kylstras wrote their flagship book, "Restoring The Foundations, an Integrated Approach to Healing Ministry." Now translated into many languages, this book became the basis for their ministry training of others.

In 2000, the Kylstras launched the Healing House Network as the covering organization for the many qualified professional Restoring The Foundations ministers who had been trained. This Network has expanded as their revelation continued to spread world-wide. At this writing, there are HHN members leading RTF in twenty nations.

In 2004, the prophecies concerning a Training Center came to fulfillment. Echo Mountain Inn in Hendersonville, NC, was purchased as the home of "Restoring The Foundations International Training Center." It became their new ministry base which has allowed a great acceleration in the preparation and release of RTF Ministers into the Body of Christ.

Healing House Network teams are being used by the Lord to minister to leaders and others in the Body of Christ, usually in an intensive one-week format. In addition, many church teams have been trained as Issue-Focused and/or Thorough Format Ministers. They are serving their local churches, volunteering three to six hours a week doing their part to prepare the Bride without spot and wrinkle.

In addition, the Kylstras have seen amazing results as they have applied the RTF principles to cleanse entire organizations, as expressed in their book "Transforming Your Organization."

In September, 2015, Chester and Betsy 'passed the baton' as leaders of Restoring The Foundations International into the very capable hands of Lee and Cindi Whitman. The Kylstras now are serving as chairman of the RTF Board of Directors, as well as Ambassadors for Restoring The Foundations Ministry.

Contact Information:
  Chester and Betsy Kylstra
  Chester@RestoringTheFoundations.org
  Betsy@RestoringTheFoundations.org
  www.PHW.org (personal ministry website)

www.ingramcontent.com/pod-product-compliance
Lightning Source LLC
Chambersburg PA
CBHW051214090426
42742CB00022B/3450